| DATE DUE | | |
|---|---|---|
| RECEIVED FEB 1 4 1996 | | |
| | | 1 2 JUN 2000 |
| JUL 1 1 1996 | | June 21/00 |
| JUL 0 4 1996 | | -1 MAR 2001 |
| JUL 0 9 1996 | | Woo 28/01 |
| SEP 3 0 1996 | | 2 9 NOV 2002 |
| Oct 10/96 | | |
| Sept 30/97 | | |

7th Street

# SUCCESSFUL
## Conference
## and
## Convention
## Planning

# SUCCESSFUL
# Conference and Convention Planning

Robert H. Drain
Neil Oakley

**McGRAW-HILL RYERSON LIMITED**

TORONTO, MONTREAL, NEW YORK, ST. LOUIS, SAN FRANCISCO,
AUCKLAND, BEIRUT, BOGOTÁ, DÜSSELDORF, JOHANNESBURG,
LISBON, LONDON, LUCERNE, MADRID, MEXICO, NEW DELHI,
PANAMA, PARIS, SAN JUAN, SÃO PAULO, SINGAPORE, SYDNEY,
TOKYO

SUCCESSFUL CONFERENCE AND CONVENTION PLANNING
Copyright © McGraw-Hill Ryerson Limited, 1978

ISBN 0-07-082609-9

1 2 3 4 5 6 7 8 9 0 D 7 6 5 4 3 2 1 0 9 8

Printed and bound in Canada




Canadian Cataloguing in Publication Data
Drain, Robert H.
   Successful conference and convention planning
ISBN 0-07-082609-9
1. Congresses and conventions.   I. Oakley,
Neil M.   II. Title.
AS6.D73              658.4'56              C78-001033-7




Designed by Brian F. Reynolds

FOR MARILYN DRAIN

FOR ROBBIE OAKLEY

# Table of Contents

# Foreword

Two of the serious, common weaknesses in public relations practice on both sides of our U.S.-Canadian border are those of aimlessness and hasty improvisation. Aimlessness is born of having a management that fails to set definite, attainable objectives for a public relations program. Hasty, jerry-built planning is usually the reflection of such aimlessness. Staging conventions, conference, and congresses is a common task in public relations practice because such events are usually designed to advance the public relations or educational objectives of the sponsors. Yet this is an assignment too often sloughed off as "routine" or else one addressed too close to convention time. Those of us who are a bit convention-weary know all too well that many conferences and conventions fail to reward those who attend; consequently such meetings fail to reward the sponsor. Most of us tend, all too easily, to fall into the rut of routine which leads to doing the same old chores in the same old ways. This human failing accounts for many of the conventions that have disappointed, conventions that were a waste of the participants' time and money, a waste of the sponsor's manpower and money, and — even more costly — an opportunity for two-way communication missed.

Bob Drain and Neil Oakley have written a readable and reliable guide to the planning and staging of a lively convention that has validity; one that has value for the participants and value for the sponsor. They know whereof they write and their writing sparkles. As a teacher, author and lecturer in public relations for more than a quarter-century I have staged many conferences and participated in hundreds.

It was my pleasure to speak to the 23rd Annual Meeting of the Canadian Public Relations Society in Winnipeg which these two authors organized. As a speaker I was carefully instructed and programmed; as a guest I was royally entertained. Never have I had a more receptive audience because I was speaking to delegates who were learning and having a good time doing it. I have never observed a more smoothly-run convention or conference. It was for this reason that I encouraged them to put their expertise into a book so it would be widely available to all of us who, at one time or another, are confronted with the awesome task of planning and staging a convention for several hundred persons.

Their "how to" manual, *Successful Conference and Convention Planning,* is a much-needed and long-overdue addition to the tools of public relations practice. The solid fundamentals of effective public relations are systematic fact-finding and feedback; careful, thoughtful planning; implementation of such plans through skilled communication and appropriate action; and, finally, evaluation of a completed project to ensure that an organization profits from its experience so the next project is more successful than the last. These same fundamentals apply to staging a successful convention or conference that has value for its participants and advances the set goals of its sponsor.

Bob Drain and Neil Oakley have followed these fundamentals in erecting the required signposts that lead to a successful convention from the time it is proposed to its evaluation by those who participated. These signposts are easy to read and easy to follow, however new to the task one may be. If their successful pattern is studied and implemented with a modicum of flair and skill, then many more sponsors will be rewarded for their investment of money and manpower in these rituals — and all of us will be spared dull, drab "going through the motions" conventions of which there are far too many.

All in all, this book represents a substantial and useful addition to the knowledge available to the public relations practitioner, trade association executive or convention planner. Thus I am happy and honored to speed the book on its way with my warm endorsement.

SCOTT M. CUTLIP,
Co-author *Effective Public Relations,*
Prentice-Hall, Englewood Cliffs, N.Y., U.S.A.

# Preface

This book is a step-by-step guide to conference and convention planning. It includes behind-the-scenes insights on research, themes and purposes, management, delegate needs, budgets, exhibits and displays, speakers, sessions and awards, family requirements, printing, promotion and publicity, services, equipment and transportation, accommodation, registration, professional assistance and media requirements.

For delegate-conscious convention chairmen and committee members, whether veterans or neophytes, it provides a compendium of useful conference techniques and ideas. Nowhere have all the responsibilities and requirements of the several parties involved in a convention been catalogued in this way and examined in one book so total interrelationships and common goals can be identified.

This book is primarily designed as a working guide for conference organizers whether experienced or involved for the first time in the planning and running of a convention delegate program — be it for business, industry, government, or recreation.

Conference working groups need all the help they can get. And they have to rely heavily on those who were originally instrumental in bringing the event to their city. Sharing concern for the event to run smoothly are the local city council, key personnel at the convention bureau, chamber of commerce, tourist association, convention complex, conference hotels, and of course, your own organization. From the beginning, it is an opportunity for good public relations carry-through and an opportunity to send out-of-town delegates home with the right impression of your city — provided the convention committee receives plenty of advance help where and when it is needed.

It's big business. Various estimates indicate that total American and Canadian expenditures on conventions and meetings of all kinds easily exceed $11 billion annually. Some $10 billion is spent in the United States alone. The remaining $1 billion accounts for a major Canadian industry, a figure that could go higher when new data is compiled from convention bureaus across the country.

Working together for mutual benefit is one way to gain control of the action. There isn't much point in beginning with a 10- or 20-person executive committee, organizing to a fault and producing a mediocre convention. Delegates can, and will, return home dissatisfied. This could well be the end of the matter, except that poorly planned conferences are rarely forgotten.

We have emphasized the need for early and thorough planning to create convention harmony and success. We hope to spark some sure-fire ideas for you, show you how to avoid pitfalls and save time and effort. If so, the following chapters have achieved their purpose — your conference will be *the* one to attend.

# Acknowledgements

We are indebted to many people for their valuable contributions as well as to those organizations that provided us with tried and workable ideas for successful conference management.

In gathering information for a work such as this, much depends on interviews with men and women who have specific know-how gained firsthand in the varied segments of the convention field.

For letters and helpful cooperation, we thank the International Association of Convention Bureaus, Cincinnati, Ohio; National Association of Home Builders, Houston Convention-Exposition, Houston, Texas; International Union of Official Travel Organizations, Geneva, Switzerland; Canadian Government Office of Tourism, Ottawa, Canada; The Conference Board, New York, N.Y.; New York Telephone Co., New York, N.Y.; British Post Office, London, England; PR Reporter, Exeter, New Hampshire; Hilton Hotels, Toronto, Canada; Hotel Fort Garry and the Tourist and Convention Association of Manitoba, Winnipeg, Canada; Capital Visitors and Convention Bureau, Ottawa, Canada.

To the innumerable individuals and associates who are not mentioned here go the warmest thanks of the authors. We would include particularly in this category the many librarians we had the privilege to contact for research assistance, all of whom were particularly helpful.

We especially acknowledge the guidance and professional support provided by Professor Scott Cutlip, University of Georgia, Athens, Georgia, whose encouragement helped make this book a reality.

# SUCCESSFUL

## Conference
## and
## Convention
## Planning

# 1

This Business of
## CONFERENCES
## AND CONVENTIONS

**W**hen the world's first conference was held, every person on earth was involved — Adam and Eve. History has shown they didn't have sufficient time or expertise to organize their program. And look at what the consequences were!

The main difference between that meeting and those held throughout the world today is that convention organization and planning has almost become a science. If you have been nominated to follow in Adam and Eve's footsteps you deserve congratulations and sympathy in large measure. The business of conferences, congresses and conventions has come a long way since the beginnings of humanity. You are stepping into a technology of rapidly increasing sophistication that today concentrates heavily on the arts of communications and interpersonal relations rather than receptions and relaxation.

Apart from this, you are about to be involved in the inner workings of a highly competitive business, one that has become a major North American industry.

Whether it is Canada or the United States, the typical national convention delegate spends $110 to $140 a day for accommodation, entertainment, refreshment, registration, trainee and personal expenditures, including gifts. Delegates attend 3½ days at the usual North American convention, but some conferences last as long as 10 days without a break. Moreover, individual round-trip travel expenses to the meeting site often exceed all other per delegate convention costs. Some sources indicate conference delegates spend twice as much per day as the average tourist.

Spending habits vary widely, of course, low for religious conventions, high for rapid-growth, production-industry sessions. But the thought of 1,000 out-of-town delegates and spouses spending at least $500,000 in less than four days has set many a city council thinking.

The result is a chilling awareness in astute cities, states and provinces that $25-to-$50-million convention centre complexes are almost a necessity. Major conventions, seeking thousands of hotel rooms, acres of meeting and exhibit space and efficient transportation must bypass the majority of American and Canadian cities which lack modern conference facilities. Some organizations, lured by sophisticated meeting and accommodation complexes, have signed 10-year conference contracts; committing themselves to return to the same city on a long-term basis. The Houston complex is a good U.S. example, while in Canada Calgary and Winnipeg have led off with multi-purpose convention centres to attract more of the conference industry. Outside the continent, the city of West Berlin is building Europe's largest convention centre with a banquet hall which seats 4,000 and a congress hall for 5,000.

The complexities of today's conventions are almost boundless. Toastmasters' convention organizers think nothing of 1,500 delegates arriving from 35 or more countries. Talk, transportation and meeting facilities tax the planners' imagination.

The Canadian Restaurant Association Annual Trade Show is by no means a major undertaking in the eyes of convention experts. Yet the CRA annually attracts an audience which exceeds 45,000 people. Running exhibit frontage is more than 60,000 linear feet. It is not a show that can be held in yesterday's exhibit halls. Ample space, sophisticated facilities and large local audiences are the prime considerations of CRA convention planners.

Total international convention business — meetings held for delegates from two or more nations — has now grown to the point that more than 4,600 people are meeting daily in all manner of international discussions. This means some 4,000 annual meetings a year on a world-wide scale, bringing together more than 1.6 million people of all nationalities. They meet for many purposes — association, corporate, academic, sales, political, promotional and public affairs. Sessions may be open or closed, some generating the major news of the day, others going almost unremarked, even by the participants.

As it is such a rapidly-changing industry, it is hard to find two experts who will agree on the definition of the terms: conferences, congresses and conventions. Conferences could perhaps be defined as mostly work and little play, conventions as having the reverse balance and congresses as a little of both — occurring when the assembled delegates represent two or more countries. Beyond that, there are symposiums, conclaves and just plain meetings. Throughout this book, conferences and conventions are used as interchangeable words, referring to annual sessions held by volunteer, professional and trade associations or private industry, including business and manufacturers.

Whatever the terminology, all these gatherings imply great demands on hotel accommodation and meeting space as well as speakers. The location, audience and event may mean speakers costing as much as $3,000, quite apart from their hotel and transportation expenses. It means early planning and preparation to minimize the competition of thousands of organizations and businesses looking forward to holding their meetings the same time as yours.

The International Union of Official Travel Organizations in Geneva, Switzerland, estimates that by 1985 international conventions will involve from 17 to 50 million people and that there could be 98,000 international congresses being held annually.

Regardless of the purpose or locale of these meetings, North American conferences have consistent attendance patterns. Recent research by the International Association of Convention Bureaus shows some 20 per cent of all conferences, congresses and conventions of a national or regional nature have less than 250 delegates. Conferences organized for 251 to 400 delegates account for 16.5 per cent; those organized for 401 to 600 delegates take in another 17 per cent. An estimated 7.9 per cent applies to gatherings with 601 to 800 delegates and 9.4 per cent for 801 to 1,000 delegates. In other words, more than 70 per cent of all major conferences attract 1,000 or fewer delegates.

This book has been written with the planning and organization guidelines in mind for the 54 per cent of all meetings which accommodate and nourish 600 or fewer delegates. But size or type doesn't really matter. When you are in this league the elements are the same whether you are experienced, or involved in running the show for the first time. It is a matter of establishing a convention budget then cutting your luncheon and dinner cloths accordingly, in keeping with the basic thoughts and ideas presented in the following chapters.

This book sets out, perhaps for the first time, how to keep a clean and cold clutch on the conference coffers — and how to make reasonable profits, if this is one of your declared objectives.

Consolidated event charts emphasize the theme that spreading the workload throughout the conference committee is the best way to cut down costs and to organize the forthcoming chaos. The idea is not to over organize, rather it is to budget and plan for education, fun and profit.

So, it's the 50th annual conference or your very first convention and you'd like to follow a formal, established program. This book shows you how to start from square one, offers you a total look at conventions and lets you live in peace with your friends. It not only tabulates convention housekeeping but also examines the essential philosophy of conferences, congresses and conventions while giving you — the planner and worker — options and choices to achieve your desired goals.

One editorial comment — every conference is different. Objectives and themes have wide variation and application. Organizational structures differ in number and purpose. No two cities or convention hotels are the same. Every statement about conferences can be modified to suit the particular convention situation which faces your committee.

Rather than generalize, frequently the liberty is taken of making definite statements. This technique has been followed throughout the book on the premise that convention planners are seeking order-out-of-chaos strategies and will apply their own judgement according to convention customs and circumstances.

First things first then. Is there a real reason for a conference? What with modern communication techniques blossoming every 24 hours and the mass media providing instant knowledge to millions every waking moment, it is wise to examine whether there are valid reasons for the proposed sessions.

If the answer is yes, then every member of every committee must approach the whole operation with the attitude that they intend to plan and manage the most successful conference ever. And the program will be complete with new ideas, attitudes and themes.

At the same time, don't overlook the fundamental premise that conferences are usually held for one of two reasons — to build increased morale and belief in the organization, or to educate delegates. Conferences, congresses and conventions are therefore merely vehicles, never ends in themselves. Success is seldom a matter of luck. Conventions must be carefully planned, well in advance, then efficiently managed from start to finish.

# 2

**Preliminary Groundwork**
## YEARS BEFORE THE FACT

ost businesses and associations select their conference sites five or more years in advance. In all probability the choice was made without the knowledge of any member of the convention's working committee. In a highly competitive business such long-range planning is essential if organizations want the best of the conference, congress and convention world.

Determining the conference site long before anyone is concerned with the selection of the conference chairman has become the rule rather than the exception. The space and accommodation crunch is so great, organizations planning 200- to 600-delegate conferences would have few convention site choices if these decisions were left to a later date.

To help you plan or organize your upcoming conference, let's review what went on years before the fact. When you understand all the decision-making that was required, you will see that selecting your city was and is quite a compliment. And, those decisions, made many years ago, now mean a challenging and rewarding experience for every committee member involved. Besides, somewhere down the road, you could be participating in the site selection process yourself. And remember, a convention means job opportunities in your city and the generating of local revenues for everything from restaurants, souvenir shops, and taxis to street vendors.

More than likely your mayor, the chamber of commerce, the tourist bureau, the convention manager and several of your senior confrères had some say in the site and date selection.

Before settling on your city as the convention location, someone was responsible for researching several basic facts and requirements well in advance. These would include usual delegate attendance, size and number of required meetings, hospitality and exhibit room needs, as well as typical return travel costs to your location.

Conference timing — and dollar savings — would be considered. The use of civic centres, arenas and other large exhibition areas would be assessed to see if the ingredients for superb convention service were there.

An intensive preliminary site investigation would be undertaken to determine the type of facility and accommodation best suited to the association's purposes. In the process, the following combinations and permutations were probably considered:

AIRPORT HOTELS: Excellent for locked-in short meetings with very little opportunity for delegate distraction. Often smaller than major hotels, so your conference will be the prime customer with all facilities at your disposal. Advantages could be offset by the remote location and access to the bright lights.

CONVENTION SITES: A comparatively recent innovation on the conference scene are hotels which cater almost exclusively to the convention business. As all the facilities are there your organization's workload is substantially reduced. Still unresolved in many hotels is one major problem — how to check 600 delegates out and 600 delegates in during the same morning or afternoon. Satisfy yourself personally on this — well ahead of time — by watching two other conventions with check-in, check-out conflict.

CRUISE SHIPS: More and more appealing to jaded conventioneers who have digested a dozen or more annual meetings in hotels new and old. Meetings rooms are limited but a good convention is guaranteed if you can book the entire vessel. Two items demand attention: an all-delegate supply of seasickness medication and awareness that costs are based on charter, not cruise rates. It's a chance to get away from it all.

FOREIGN HOTELS: A recent newspaper advertisement states: "It only takes an hour and a half from New York to fly your convention back into the 17th century." It's an interesting change that works, provided income tax regulations permit, no revolutions are underfoot, and foreign locales provide gourmet eating experiences. North American chain hotels in far-off lands combine the best of all worlds and private plumbing. Language barriers are not a problem.

MAJOR HOTELS: Usually heart-of-city operations with full facilities and amenities nearby. The size of your conference in relation to the number of rooms in the hotel is important. A relatively small conference in a large hotel can be more than awkward if the hotel management has booked in three other conventions at the same time — each larger than yours.

RESORT HOTELS: Earn top ratings for long meetings, large-family attendance and minimum distracting factors. Usually have generous off-season rates that make family attendance quite attractive. Most resort hotels also get high marks for personalized staff service to all delegates. Moreover, one continues to be amazed at the excellent, self-contained convention staff capability in the regular, remote-resort hotels. Distractions can be a problem. How are you going to keep delegates out of the pool or off the golf course?

UNIVERSITY CAMPUSES: For the quiet, research-orientated program, nothing comes close to the environment created on North America's modern university campus settings. New dormitories often have private washrooms and striking architecture. Food costs and accommodation rates are generally well below those offered by hotels and resorts in the immediate vicinity. Spartan menus, scarcity of refreshments and utilitarian atmosphere may not be suitable if delegates show a preference for high living.

Large or small — new or old — convention hotels are strictly a matter of preference, best decided by taking delegates' needs into consideration. But the key to this choice is to hire experienced hotel management. If the hotel isn't built yet, let some other organization sponsor the opening convention. Hotel experts say it takes six months and a 30-per-cent staff turnover before a hotel can responsibly handle a major conference.

No matter what hotel site you like, the basics must be kept in mind. Inspect the premises personally. How well does the front desk operate when 30 or more delegates are checking in at the same moment? Ask to see a few guest rooms, the best suite and the meeting rooms. Observe a few meetings in progress to see if a pleasant atmosphere has been achieved. Have a full-course meal and check the quality and service.

Be anonymous at this point. It is better if people are unaware of your purposes. But talk to any and all staff you see — bellmen, housekeepers and dining room staff — to determine their attitudes and work habits. The manager won't have time to personally attend to even one of your delegates. It is the staff who handle this important responsibility.

If everything appears to be in order it's finally time to tip your hand to the local convention bureau. Bureau staff can determine in confidence if hotel space is available coincident with your planned convention date several years hence. They can also provide you with data and printed materials plus suggestions as to the most suitable time of year and time of week. Many convention bureaus also provide convention planning tips and courtesies.

Selling the proposal to the national organization was not difficult, but again it was a series of step-by-step efforts to increase the possibilities. The following factors were an instrumental part of the process which brought the conference to your city.

Convince key delegates long before the decision is to be made.

Detail pertinent facts only, committing yourselves to events you know you can deliver. Overselling kills the best-laid plans.

Stress the reasons for coming to your city and refuse to comment on program or theme. Who knows what will happen to the organization during the next two to four years?

Stress the fact you can plan a convention and organize an efficient, active and aggressive conference committee.

Forget all reference to past successes or failures and comparisons between your convention and the one currently in session.

Package your proposal. You need to be armed with kits and visual material. It is wise to consider convention bureau, city hall as well as provincial or state officials as part of the package.

Convention floor presentations are best because they generate early delegate awareness. Lining up audience acceptance prior to the event is often beneficial and it implies a spontaneous approval.

Whatever you plan, the organization must believe everyone wants to hold the convention in your community.

If there are two or three alternate conference site possibilities, it is worthwhile for conference-locale seekers to develop a grading sheet of delegate preferences.

| LOCATION | SITE No. 1 | SITE No. 2 | SITE No. 3 | PREFERENCE |
|---|---|---|---|---|
| Airport Hotel | | | | |
| Convention Hotel | | | | |
| Cruise Ship | | | | |
| Downtown Hotel | | | | |
| Foreign Hotel | | | | |
| Resort Hotel | | | | |
| Suburban Hotel | | | | |
| University Campus | | | | |
| Civic Centre, Arena | | | | |

Thoroughly check each of the following for convenience and a well-maintained condition:

## ACCESS ☐
Amenities
Parking
Shops
Transportation

## CONFERENCE FACILITIES ☐
Banquet Rooms
Bedrooms
Elevators
Exhibit Halls
Lobby
Meeting Rooms

## MEETING ROOMS ☐
Access
Air Conditioning
Lighting
Noise Control
Number
Registration Space
Sizes
Sound System

## BANQUET ROOMS ☐
Access
Air Conditioning
Lighting
Noise Control
Number
Seating Arrangements
Sizes
Sound System

## EXHIBIT HALL ☐
Access
Air Conditioning
Exhibit Power Sources
Exhibit Unit Sizes
Floor Space
Lighting
Noise Control
Sound System

## BEDROOMS ☐
Air Conditioning
Average Room Rate
Bathroom Facilities
Colored Television
Furniture Condition
Number Bedsitting Rooms
Number Double Bedrooms
Number Hospitality Rooms
Number Single Bedrooms
Number Suites

## SITE MANAGEMENT ☐
Billing/Payment
Cashier
Check-In Times
Check-Out Times
Executive Attitudes

Front Desk
Laundry/Dry Cleaning
Room Service
Staff Attitudes

Knowing the preliminary planning involved in landing a convention provides good insight for the working conference team as it follows through with detailed research. The positive and enthusiastic acceptance of your site some years beforehand sets the stage and can only enhance your convention. Make the most of these well-planned beginnings.

# Conference Research for
# PURPOSE AND PROFIT

**N**ow that the conference is in your hands the first planning priority must be basic research. Conference objectives and themes will be one of your immediate concerns. A detailed examination of the history of the sponsoring group as well as a review of current influences and future goals are the most reliable techniques to ensure everything relevant falls into place during the months ahead. Research will tell you a great deal, including what the conference's basic themes and objectives should eventually be to create maximum delegate involvement.

All research is best undertaken by a preliminary planning committee, one which manages and co-ordinates all information. It should be disbanded without hesitation when its report is complete so any continuing influence is held to a minimum during later planning stages. The job is to survey a membership sample to determine likes, dislikes, attitudes, attendance, accommodation requirements, basic program, session and special event aims.

Such membership surveys are fraught with danger and determining a valid sample is very difficult. It is so easy to assume the membership in an association automatically means an audience of delegates with a single mind. The reverse is probably true. Certainly, in every organization there is a wide range of ages, backgrounds, local environments, levels of responsibility, experience, and particularly attitudes — pro and con — about current membership concerns. Sampling can only have relevance and validity when it is designed to accommodate the differences of potential attendees. Above all, every sample survey — regardless of measurement technique — must be designed to yield reliable opinions. Otherwise you risk generating confused rather than constructive data. One of the best techniques for conference purposes is the "first person survey" approach. "What-do-you-think-of" questions are replaced by "I believe that" statements to yield a far more personal evaluation than the norm.

Paramount to convention opinion sampling is the need to separate data from delegates, establishing the number of conventions attended in the past. Veterans of 10 conventions are more informed, and perhaps more reliable, than individuals who are about to attend a conference for the first time. Nevertheless, conference initiates will probably have some fresh and interesting ideas your preliminary planning committee should consider.

So, every questionnaire requires space for delegate identity — apart from name — and then several questions along the following lines:

- Sessions I liked last year included ...........................
...............................................................

- I really didn't like ........................................
...............................................................

- If I had the opportunity, I'd like to attend sessions covering ....
...............................................................

- I'd like less attention paid to ...............................
...............................................................

- I'm partial to formal .... informal .... sessions.

- In my opinion, our organization's major problem today is ......
...............................................................
and our biggest challenge in the next five years is ............
...............................................................

- Opinion leaders I'd like to hear at the next conference include ..
......................................................
......................................................

- Accommodation that best suits me includes ..................
......................................................

- And I hope to pay no more than $.................. per night
$.................., if my family attends.

- Time of year, month and week I prefer .....................
......................................................

- If there was a good spouses' program I probably would ......
wouldn't ...... invite my husband/wife to the convention.

- If you guaranteed an excellent children's program, at minimum
cost, I would...... wouldn't...... bring them along.

- I prefer the following convention site:
Airport Hotel...... Convention Hotel...... Cruise Ship......
Foreign Hotel...... Major Downtown Hotel...... Resort Hotel
...... University Campus.......

- If I were organizing our next conference, these are the changes
and innovations I would make .............................
......................................................
......................................................
......................................................
......................................................
......................................................
......................................................
......................................................
......................................................
......................................................

Remember though anyone who seeks opinion in today's world and then ignores it is a fool tempting fate. The best policy is to have one person analyze the data and then present it to the committee. It has been said before: a committee of three automatically guarantees four opinions — and little opportunity to match programs to people.

Survey opinions have to be augmented by data from other sources. Check what other organizations have found successful in the past several months. Do random interviews by telephone, hand or ballot. Hold several critique sessions amongst potential conference committee members and keep your own eyes, ears and minds open.

Attendance audits and audience-interest questionnaires completed during and after the previous conference are a valuable windfall. Feedback is fairly reliable but you must ensure you know the circumstances under which these checks were made. People object to being overly surveyed and such material might well be distorted.

In any event, data analysts should be prepared to accept and even be surprised by conference survey findings, especially when the data conveys varying opinions in the light of previous conferences. If something goes against all that's traditional — take heed. What is past is past and some radical program changes probably have to be made.

The committee has to set new standards for your conference. Why risk continued or fresh criticism when accolades are so much better?

Research data, properly interpreted, is the prime lever to change in established thinking. New data can justify change in dates, change in locale, change in objectives and themes, to say nothing of change in imagination. Opinion unsupported by data is usually blunted by outspoken, subjective opinion. And weak research generally opens the floodgates of personal bias.

There are, after all, many valid reasons for change, and preliminary planning committees need to be aware of these factors if they wish to propose worthwhile advance plans for a meaningful conference. Avoid planning complacency. Watch for the following obvious signals which will indicate change is imminent:

New technology within the association or corporate enterprise
Introduction of new product or process
New economic, sociological or political era
New organization policy or legislation
Declining delegate attendance
Delegate revolt — if things have reached that stage!

# 4

## Where to Find
# INSTANT HELP AND IDEAS

**T**hink of the conference location as being a new environment where delegates can escape current cares and concerns. The preliminary planning committee's ultimate charge then is to suggest a program where discussion and dialogue can be analyzed in their proper context, in keeping with the delegates' needs and the site itself. The modern information flow is so extensive and the world so complex, delegates can no longer sit in isolation and determine unified action. The conference can provide the vehicle to develop human resolution of problems and to foster unified points of view, provided these objectives are firmly entrenched in preliminary convention planning.

So, you can't simply research your audience and get all your convention planning completed in a matter of days. Remember, your delegates are a multitude of different personalities.

Today's conferences suffer problems of scale and outside experts are often required—if only in an advisory capacity—to simplify and rationalize the recommendations under consideration. Too often conventions

uch talking, too much information, too many sessions
d sometimes, too many conferences and conventions.
tlessness, fatigue and frustration. There are definite
mber of convention days and hours. Beyond these
become spectators and conference collapse sets in.
e hazards, experienced committees seek out several
essional organizations in the conference, congress and
convention ness to bring sound advice to hand. In addition, there
is a good selection of consultants available, knowledgeable in one or
more of the special activities typically occurring at a convention.

Most professionals will advise that the real secret of convention
organizing lies in being able to isolate the purpose of the meeting,
the general theme and the people who will be involved on the conference floor. Once these three elements are clearly identified, it only
remains to manage the simple tasks—development of specific programs
and proposals to achieve basic objectives.

If funds are available for preliminary research, you should consider
asking the following convention service specialists for proposals and
ideas.

| | |
|---|---|
| Advertising Agencies | Florist Suppliers |
| Audio-Visual Consultants | Furniture Rental Companies |
| Cartage Companies | Management Consultants |
| Conference Badge Manufacturers | Media Relations Consultants |
| Conference Supply Houses | Model, Talent Agencies |
| Convention Bureaus | Photographic Specialists |
| Convention Hostess Services | Public Relations Consultants |
| Convention Management Firms | Registration Bureaus |
| Decoration Supply Houses | Sales and Marketing Personnel |
| Exhibit Display Firms | Trade Show Consultants |
| Film Producers | Transportation Representatives |
| | Travel Agencies |

How you use this outside expertise, and to what extent, depends upon
projected attendance, delegate sophistication, importance of objectives
and how much there is to spend. For short-duration conferences only
the odd piece of rented audio-visual equipment may be involved. On
the other hand, if a good film is the answer consult professionals who
can provide or produce a quality film to suit specific needs. For three-
day conventions, involving 400 or more delegates, some organizations
expect to commit 10 per cent of the conference budget for communications tools provided by professional firms.

Time and time again it has been proven that expert assistance in
conference planning more than outweighs the costs involved. But be
fair to yourselves and your consultants. Professional convention pack-
aging is seldom possible in low-budget conference situations.

Reputable organizations in the convention planning field review needs in keeping with the budget and suggest several cost options and packages. Consultants can run the entire conference or provide specialized services. They also know how to research as well as evaluate and write conference planning reports. Invite proposals in writing from as many sources as necessary, requesting written bids for opening on a pre-determined date along with experience resumes. The proposal-bid technique usually eliminates talkers from workers and provides clear indication of conference expertise.

Good bids set out possible objectives and several options for those elements where professional assistance is really required. Work-hours, services, timing, and on-the-job responsibilities must be clearly detailed, together with total cost options, in keeping with the scale of consultant services required. Only when all bids and support data are evaluated is it time to enter into agreements. But remember, someone has to control the conference consultants and experts or planning and costs could get out of hand when least expected. Firm-price consultant contracts—in writing—are essential.

If the preliminary planning committee believes the organization's interests are best served by hiring consultants, then that is the route to take. On the other hand, the majority of conferences are organized by people who are handling this task for the first time. A successful conference can be organized with non-professional staff. Keep in mind, too, that hotel staff and convention centres offer many of their advisory services free. It is wrong to expect them to lend you staff but they are highly experienced in several areas relevant to conference needs and usually more than willing to help.

Preliminary planning should now be almost complete and what is required at this stage is a series of recommendations.

- ☐ Whether or not to proceed
- ☐ Potential delegate attendance and profile
- ☐ Recommended conference dates
- ☐ Conference objective and theme considerations
- ☐ Outline of possible work session alternatives
- ☐ Special problems and concerns
- ☐ Overall budget estimate
- ☐ Recommended consultant and services options

The recommendations will also include an analysis of conference benefits versus costs. They possibly may even suggest a more economic method of achieving basic objectives.

If, for example, your conference is on unemployment or one organized to mount a campaign for funds, posh surroundings are contrary to your objectives. Seek the inexpensive setting.

# 5

**Trials and Tribulations of**
# CONFERENCE CHAIRMEN

**S**electing a chairman is much more than just appointing the first available person. For openers, imposing a chairmanship could mean buying a barrel of committee differences, difficulties, and discontent.

Good chairmen have a past record of getting things done with a maximum of goodwill. They have the ability to command respect and the knack of getting along with others. Ideally, chairmen are courted by hotel, airline, convention and local authorities who want and seek his or her business. Successful leaders are not just democratic in the normal sense, they encourage discussion and stimulate people to work in harmony. They know how to handle people tactfully and impartially; setting the example by being working chairmen and providing leadership. These individuals make tasks and people happen in concert—transforming planning rhetoric into conference reality.

In North America, it means looking for a person who believes in total delegation of responsibility and who has a talent to make this philosophy work. American and Canadian committee people are primarily joiners and doers. They love to get involved as long as they know what is required and are given real responsibility. In a sense they are co-workers, not employees. Conference committee personnel may often hold positions in the community more senior than that of the chairman. The onus for unity and harmony in the organization is therefore on the chairman. If the committee is chaired by a person of sincerity who possesses a clear sense of direction all can play their roles in creating the conference without status hangups.

On the other hand, most European chairmen—together with their steering or executive committees—have total control over all conference planning decisions. Essentially, the role of committee workers is to implement a previously determined program. Each system has merits within its particular context.

A good chairman has to know the worth of each committee member and be able to recognize the worth of innovative concepts. Otherwise, it's the same old, dull, boxed-in convention. It is a case of listening to committee ideas and appreciating the merits of outside experts as well as knowing how to translate thoughts into action.

The entire conference operation revolves around the conference chairman. So much so, no chairman can afford to become swallowed up in details and personalities. The job is the nourishment of the conference structure as a whole. The committee's leader must lead a healthy unit so the team continues to survive all future pressures. New ideas must be tried out and researched, but the good chairman keeps them from being bogged down in discussion.

Perhaps the most common cause of sleepless nights for chairmen of conventions, regardless of size, is the problem of the committee worker who does not fulfill his or her responsibilities. It's best solved by finding new slots on the team, better suited to the talents of the individuals concerned. There is little doubt this is the biggest burden borne by any chairman and the longer it is left unresolved, the weaker the whole team effort becomes. If the situation arises tackle it without hesitation so other committee members continue to function with maximum efficiency.

Efficient conference management demands prompt solutions to internal problems of this kind. In addition it means the appointment of a co-chairman who can readily recognize trouble areas and tackle detail—at a moment's notice. If you tend to be an imaginative and colorful individual try to find your opposite in a co-chairman. Let everybody know you operate as a team—but you are the single spokesman. You will maximize the best of both worlds in the process.

Co-chairmen have to play a rigid, behind-the-scenes role. They are experts who can detail and outline hundreds of activities, weaving them together in a comprehensive plan. The co-chairman has to be able to step in, recommend, plan and program improvements without hesitation, detailing every step along the way.

Most important of all, the chairman must manage people and the co-chairman must manage events. In the final analysis, it is the chairman who sells the events to the committees concerned.

It almost goes without saying the appointment of two chairmen with equal authority, each responsible for half the committees and half the operations is sheer suicide. Unfortunately, it is done too often, usually with the rationale that the load is too big for one person. The end result is virtually guaranteed—a major power vacuum.

Chairmen and co-chairmen live, sleep, eat and breathe convention budgets. Someone, somewhere, has to pay for everything. It is best to know where the money will come from, long before the conference starts. So right from the beginning, both the chairman and the co-chairman are involved in expenses and revenue as well as programming, promotion, accommodation and the selection and management of an organization of sensitive individuals.

Having said this, there are two other essentials basic to successful chairman and co-chairmanship. Ideally, both should live in the same city so they can achieve maximum operational communication. Moreover, their employers must fully agree to their appointments and the time demands involved. Few conventions succeed if the principal organizers lack full freedom of time and travel during the several months leading up to the conference.

In North America, where the executive committee customarily functions as a coordinating board of individual conference committees it is important that related committee endeavors be synchronized. Certain committee functions have definite, integrated relationships and can easily be grouped, responsible to the executive committee. The following executive makeup is typical of an efficient committee grouping:

- [ ] Finance, registration, sponsorships, awards
- [ ] Program, speakers, events, entertainment, workshops
- [ ] Accommodation, services, transportation, displays
- [ ] Secretariat, news, promotion, publicity, translation

It is most important that executive committee members' functions are not confined to planning and coordinating. Each should also run one working committee and actually be in charge of one segment of the conference organizational team. This principle continues the working executive concept vested in the chairman and the co-chairman.

Executive committee members should be selected by the conference chairman, without outside influence. If all live in the same community, communication advantages increase tenfold. Large national or international conferences often require executive committees representative of several communities and interests, because the host society or chapter rarely has a sufficient pool of experienced workers. This is fair enough, but it is all the more reason for chairmen and co-chairmen to reside in the same city, preferably the convention site itself.

In any event, executive committees—North American style—serve the conference chairman and undertake active handling of most planning functions. In total-delegation-of-responsibility situations, the typical executive committee member resolves questions affecting two or more of his or her sub-committees, without reference to the entire executive or the chairman. Where the decision affects several sub-committees, then perhaps two or three executive committee members are involved. The goal is always, of course, to solve every situation at the working committee level.

Good executive committees work directly to the conference goals, laying the groundwork for the overall conference plan and organization. No matter how informal conference plans may be, trouble can be avoided by the simple policy of executive committee coordination and resolution. This technique ensures that the final conference plan and operation reflects the conclusions and decisions originally envisioned. Executive committees bog down when involved with regular day-to-day decisions. These are best left in the hands of the working committees.

Perhaps your conference has been operated over the years through a national "standing committee" system. It means experienced executive assistance for local conference committee planners. On the other hand, remember you may have to contend with some standing committee members quite opposed to change.

And there are interesting ramifications to consider in situations where there is heavy involvement by association or corporate head office staff, as opposed to the local convention committee team. Usually the crunch is felt in those areas concerning policy, planning or operations. In some national organizations, permanent head office staff is a godsend. Others provide far less than they promise.

No matter what the overriding situation is, it has to be checked in detail by the chairman and co-chairman. At the very least, obtain frank opinions from organizers on head office staff leadership and its on-the-spot performance. Depending upon your findings, you may have to arrange a detailed agreement on the division of responsibilities.

In the final analysis, how well the chairman's authority is accepted by all committee members is commensurate with how the conference will succeed. Neutrality in a chairman is rarely a good thing. Listening and developing agreement between others is what is required, along with the ability to make all agreements work. And good chairmen keep the conference organization very flexible. They shuffle and reshuffle materials, time, tools, talent and money until a fine balance is achieved.

## EXECUTIVE COMMITTEE RESPONSIBILITY CHART

| Executive Committee | Working Committees |
|---|---|
| FINANCE DIRECTOR | Finance, Registration Sponsorships, Hosting |
| PROGRAM DIRECTOR | Program, Work Sessions, Speakers, Awards, Family, Entertainment |
| ACCOMMODATION DIRECTOR | Accommodation, Meals, Meeting Rooms, Displays/Exhibits |
| SECRETARY | Minutes/Proceedings, News Media/News Conferences, Information/Translation/Printing, Service/Equipment/Transport, Post-Conference Evaluation |

CHAIRMAN

CO-CHAIRMAN

# 6

## Selecting and Setting
# THEMES AND OBJECTIVES

**L**ack of conference research is typically matched by a lack of conference objectives. It is interesting to observe how often conference planning teams devote less than a second's thought to determining objectives and goals. Be that as it may, specific things must happen at every conference and others must be avoided at all cost. Coordinated leadership and programming minimize convention disasters.

Argue if you will, but there are only two basic goals to all conferences and conventions. One is the desire to achieve specific association or management objectives. The second is the provision of audience rewards.

The fact that the conference is the regular annual meeting isn't enough justification in itself to accomplish association or management goals. What are the concerns of the organization? What external influences are affecting the future of the group? What new product or new technology is in the offing? How do you plan meetings that will ensure the continued health and stability of the organization?

Moreover, audience or delegate rewards mean much more than a gift to every attendee. Delegates should be attending the conference to exchange and pool information or to achieve action on the basis of group decisions. These two reasons can be further broken down into audience rewards such as clarifying issues, report preparation, policy formation, negotiation, support generation, education and information exchange, in addition to awards and ceremonies.

It follows that association/management goals and audience rewards are quite opposite to each other. Nevertheless, they both must be identified and fulfilled if your conference is to be a success. Indeed, the two basic goals are so separate in nature they must be considered individually in planning sessions. What will the organization accomplish at the forthcoming conference? How will the audience benefit from the proceedings?

The two-goal theory can be applied to any situation, as follows:

| VEHICLE | GOAL #1 | GOAL #2 |
|---|---|---|
| Sales Meeting: | Introduction new product | Increased sales commissions |
| Annual Meeting: | Amendment of constitution | Receipt of annual rewards |
| Church Sessions: | Increased membership | Spiritual growth |
| Political Convention: | Media exposure | Participation in the party |

Goal development techniques are obvious. Go back to intensive research amongst those who can provide the answers. A questionnaire may be of help, provided it is circulated to a cross-section of people representative of all factions within an organization. Conference objectives have to be based on the realities of the organization's requirements and delegates' needs.

The situation may be one where, as chairman, it is best to formulate objectives on your own, then develop and present a report to the executive committee for review. Whatever the approach, complete data preparation is essential so the report will be considered objectively and goals established with a minimum of bias.

Once broad objectives are firmly fixed the conference begins to assume dimension for the first time. The objectives will take on added meaning through researching the proposed convention theme.

Themes are not objectives, they merely create atmosphere and mood. Themes demonstrate to every speaker, panelist and delegate the main thrust of the conference. Conversely, a vague theme or no theme at all means confusion, lack of coordination and a blurring of the essential meeting purposes. Above all, *The 21st Annual Conference* or its equivalent, is hardly a challenging theme. *Changing Technology in the 80s* has a more valid message for all concerned.

It shouldn't be forgotten that the purpose of a theme is to generate positive delegate attitudes and involvement before, during and after the conference. Implicated are pre-conference promotion, the conference setting and post-conference evaluation.

However, be careful to ensure that the theme fits the content, never the reverse. If content has to be tailored to· fit your theme the theme isn't right for the purpose.

The first consideration in theme selection is evolving a slogan and a symbol—in keeping with the occasion. A religious theme is hardly appropriate at an industrial show, any more than *Fun in 81!* would be fitting for an ecclesiastical gathering. Go back to basics. Goals and objectives indicate the conference content, the theme reinforces the objectives.

Good conference and convention themes meet the following criteria:

> Rarely, if ever, controversial
> Unify and give continuity to entire program
> Readily identifiable and universally acceptable
> Imply action on behalf of all delegates
> Topical as well as exciting to the imagination
> Project the dignity of the organization
> Indicate change and purpose
> Reflect delegate and organization goals
> Stress business and education rather than relaxation and entertainment

All these requirements imply development of a theme with legitimate impact. The obvious or imitative theme is immediately apparent. Successful themes take time to develop. Using someone else's theme rarely pays dividends. It only demonstrates lack of imagination. Gag themes are self-destructive. They seldom enhance the image of the organization.

Consider a theme with logos and symbols in mind. Consultants are excellent in this area of conference planning and can provide invaluable assistance. But if yours is a low-budget conference there are several books covering the subject of logos and symbols readily available at most libraries. Select up-to-date editions with current ideas. Remember, too, that the logo must be readily identifiable, whether yours is a regional or international meeting. Color emphasis and typeface selection are also important. Keep in mind the fact that the logo must appear on banners, perhaps 25-feet long and 5-feet deep. Reduced logos, even down to postage stamp size will be needed on letterheads, envelopes, tickets, name badges and other small conference items.

Keep the logo design clean. Combine two or three basic elements at most in the final product. Stress the organization and the theme, or the theme and the locale.

Use of the theme and logo is vital during the last year leading up to the conference. Badges, hats, banners, exhibits, displays, slides, films, mailers and other promotion pieces fit into this category. What you are doing is repeating, repeating, repeating conference goals and themes at every opportunity to promote interest in the basic objectives of your convention.

## EXECUTIVE COMMITTEE CHECKLIST

Determine Conference Goals ☐
Determine Audience Goals ☐
Determine Conference Objectives ☐
Determine Conference Themes ☐
Determine Conference Logo ☐

# 7

## The Convention
## PLAN AND
## ORGANIZATION

**S**ome senior conference organizers develop the organization structure, assign tasks and expect the working committee chairmen and members to develop the conference program without any future guidance. Undoubtedly conferences can be organized in this manner but the cart should never come before the horse.

It remains the duty of the conference chairman and co-chairman to develop the preliminary program plan and conference budget. Founded on basic themes and objectives, it is then reviewed with the Executive Committee.

Preliminary program planning is relatively easy. The number of conference days are known, the potential audience is fairly well established and the conference objectives are defined. It is a matter of developing a bare outline program of events and sessions which will generally take up most of the waking hours of every working day.

The object is to determine all the items which can be concluded successfully—provided funds, time and staff are available. It means shooting for the maximum number of events and sessions; then in the coming months adjusting your sights as alternate ideas are proposed which will keep the conference closer to budget. In fact, you are better off planning ambitious sessions and events at the preliminary stages. High committee enthusiasm can make the impossible—or a good substitute—work. Very few suggestions made in the final weeks of the conference planning process will see the light of day on the convention floor.

Assuming registration is scheduled to begin on Tuesday evening with farewells on Saturday morning your preliminary planning could be based on a convention format such as the following:

| Tuesday | 9:00 a.m. - 5:00 p.m. | Executive Council Sessions |
|---|---|---|
| | 7:00 p.m. - 9:00 p.m. | Registration |
| | 7:00 p.m. - 9:00 p.m. | Reception |
| Wednesday | 8:00 a.m. - 9:30 a.m. | Opening Breakfast |
| | 9:00 a.m. - 9:00 p.m. | Registration |
| | 9:00 a.m. - 9:00 p.m. | Information Center |
| | 9:00 a.m. - 9:00 p.m. | News Room |
| | 10:00 a.m. - 11:00 a.m. | Youth Event |
| | 10:00 a.m. - 12:00 noon | Executive Council Sessions |
| | 12:00 noon - 12:30 p.m. | Reception |
| | 12:30 p.m. - 1:45 p.m. | Luncheon/Speaker |
| | 2:30 p.m. - 5:00 p.m. | Delegate Sessions |
| | 2:30 p.m. - 4:00 p.m. | Spouses' Event |
| | 2:30 p.m. - 10:00 p.m. | Youth Event |
| | 6:00 p.m. - 8:30 p.m. | Dinner/Speaker |
| | 9:00 p.m. - 12:00 p.m. | Annual Ball |
| Thursday | 7:30 a.m. - 9:00 a.m. | Out-of-Hotel Breakfast |
| | 9:00 a.m. - 12:00 noon | Annual Meeting |
| | 9:00 a.m. - 2:00 p.m. | Non-Voting Delegate Event |
| | 9:00 a.m. - 5:00 p.m. | Registration |
| | 9:00 a.m. - 9:00 p.m. | Information Center |
| | 9:00 a.m. - 9:00 p.m. | News Room |
| | 12:30 p.m. - 2:15 p.m. | Luncheon/Speaker |
| | 2:30 p.m. - 5:00 p.m. | Delegate Sessions |
| | 5:30 p.m. - 6:30 p.m. | Reception |
| | 7:00 p.m. - 9:30 p.m. | Dinner/Awards |
| | 7:00 p.m. - 9:30 p.m. | Youth Event |
| Friday | 8:00 a.m. - 9:30 a.m. | Hotel Breakfast |
| | 9:00 a.m. - 11:30 a.m. | Executive Council Sessions |
| | 9:30 a.m. - 11:30 a.m. | Out-of-Hotel Sessions |
| | 9:00 a.m. - 9:00 p.m. | Information Center |
| | 9:00 a.m. - 5:00 p.m. | News Room |
| | 11:30 a.m. - 1:30 p.m. | Out-of-Hotel Lunch |
| | 2:00 p.m. - 4:00 p.m. | Delegate Sessions |
| | 5:30 p.m. - 6:30 p.m. | Reception |

|          | 7:00 p.m. - 9:30 p.m.   | Annual Dinner/Speaker |
|----------|-------------------------|-----------------------|
| Saturday | 9:00 a.m. - 11:00 a.m.  | Farewell Breakfast    |

Many variations of the draft program can be considered. It can be argued that your conference should commence on Saturday and end on Tuesday. Executive sessions could be held one or two days in advance. Perhaps they are not needed. If you have specialist or sectional sessions to consider ensure that they are included in your first program draft.

As a point of interest, experience has shown last-night annual balls can be a letdown. Better to schedule them as a get-acquainted event at the very start of the conference. By the last evening, delegates have met most of the people they want to contact. Final nights usually see groups of delegates out on the town, leaving the conference committee with an empty convention hall.

The purpose of detailing the draft program at this stage is primarily to catalogue all the events and sessions. This will, in turn, indicate the potential size and number of your working committees.

The secret of working committees is to spread the workload. Committees should consist of four or five people at most. If a committee has too heavy a workload determine where a logical division might exist. Each work group should have equal power, respect and authority. And, if out-of-town committee representation is a must, place at least one local member on each committee so there is a strong communication link.

Planners who have developed a draft program are probably looking at the following areas of responsibility for working committees:

    Accommodation
    Awards
    Displays/Exhibits
    Entertainment/Events
    Finance
    Hosting
    Information/Translation/Printing
    Meals
    Meeting Rooms
    Media/News Conferences/Promotion
    Minutes/Proceedings
    Post-Conference Evaluation
    Program
    Registration
    Services/Equipment/Transport
    Speakers
    Sponsorships
    Spouses
    Work Sessions
    Youth

Hopefully, 20 committees are not required to run your conference. The point is that these are the 20 main areas of responsibility which must be covered by every committee-structure plan. Depending on the size of the convention, committees might combine and cover their responsibilities as follows:

> Accommodation/Meals/Meeting Rooms
> Awards/Displays/Exhibits/Entertainment Events
> Finance/Sponsorships
> Hosting/Registration/Spouses/Youth
> Information/Translation/Printing/Minutes/Proceedings/Post-
>     Conference Evaluation
> Media/News Conferences/Promotion
> Program/Speakers/Work Sessions
> Services/Equipment/Transportation

Note that no matter how you group the working committee structure, the Finance/Sponsorships group is so important that it should be kept separate and apart from all other responsibilities. This is the unit which is crucial to the whole operation. The conference must operate on a break-even or profit basis and financial control is vital to overall success.

The purpose of the organization plan is further amplified by detailing the responsibilities of each working committee. The majority of people are willing to volunteer for committee work but they have a right to know what will be required of them. Detailed assignments also separate responsibilities. Using this approach the Program Committee might find itself responsible for the following:

> Pre-convention assignment deadlines
> Convention manual
> Convention time schedule
> Advance, and final programs

Note, however, that the Information/Translation/Printing Committee is responsible for receipt of all Program Committee material and putting each item into print. Services/Equipment/Transport Committee members would see that the printed material is distributed to the appropriate committees as required. Such a division of responsibilities, at first glance, appears to complicate convention operations, yet the reverse is true. Keeping committee responsibilities separate avoids overlaps. Spread the work load and ensure each committee is responsible for specific functions.

Now, with a draft plan and the working committee structure on paper, it's time for executive committee review. Look for ways of improving all proposals and expanding the plan and structure. It is also the appropriate moment to group the working committees under individual executive committee representatives, according to mutual consensus. But remember, the object is to improve the plan and structure. Once approval is given you can begin to develop the convention manual.

There is continuing controversy associated with the production of convention manuals. Properly and inexpensively prepared, they can be quick reference guides for imaginative, motivated individuals. The basic working tool of every successful conference operation, the manual's first function is to enable the conference chairman to recruit aggressive and dependable working staff. In turn, the staff readily can become informed of all objectives and proposals. What is needed is a document which enables everyone to work together, fully aware of all conference details.

With these thoughts in mind the manual should contain the following material, summarized, of course, for easy readability:

> Convention goals and objectives
> Convention themes
> Draft program
> Draft budget
> Draft organization structure
> Draft committee responsibilities
> Staff names, telephone numbers, addresses

The manual should be an inexpensive, loose-leaf binder. There will be several replacement pages issued over the coming months, quite apart from any additions. It should be tabulated and sufficient copies issued so that every person down to the working committee chairman level has a personal copy.

The first draft of the convention manual is best prepared by the conference chairman and co-chairman. They alone have the task of recruiting working committee chairmen and members; a complicated process for large conferences where the committees usually are recruited on a nation-wide basis.

There are several sources to check when beginning the recruiting process. Respect nominations from senior representatives across the country and the executive committee. Look to member companies who will offer staff — even a whole committee team. Very active association members are often good choices. Young prospects, short on experience, thrive on action-packed, high-workload committees.

Obviously, local members are best recruited for vital, on site committees including Services/Equipment/Transport, Finance/Sponsorships, Accommodation, Hosting, Translation, Printing and Media/News Conferences/Promotion. These are difficult jobs to manage miles away from the conference site.

No matter where working committee chairmen and members come from — your own office or the other side of the country — selection guidelines are the same. Good working committee people have the following attributes:

> Strong supporters of the organization
> Capable of meeting objectives
> Willing, interested volunteers
> Prepared to work with others
> Decision makers and accepters
> Determination and dependability

Review the draft organization structure according to individual abilities and personalities. This people-selection process must not sacrifice the efficiency of the structure. And by all means, find a role for everyone determined to serve.

With the convention manual updated as much as possible and the nominated personnel in mind, it is now time to recruit your working chairmen. This is best done by personal contact. It's a sensitive, two-way situation. The potential working chairman has a right to know the responsibility, expense and time involved. The conference chairman has the right to ensure each working chairman is capable of handling the job. And both parties have the right to ask questions in the process. Moreover, seek company or organization agreement if time and travel are essential to the performance of the task.

Face-to-face recruitment, with a well-prepared convention manual in hand, is the sure-fire way to gather a good conference staff. Low-budget conventions rarely have travel funds available for recruiting purposes, but it is best to try to make as many personal visits as possible. At least write a detailed letter, backing it up with necessary conference outline material. It will minimize organizational grief in the months ahead.

Once all the working committee chairmen are selected, revise the convention manual and send the amendments to everyone concerned. This will begin to knit the committees into the organization structure. Each working committee chairman will require assistance in recruiting the number of working members he or she feels necessary to handle the assignments. First selections are found among those individuals unavailable for chairmanship posts because of business or other pressures.

Committees function best when there is a balance between planning and working members. And, committees should be divided into equal-authority subgroups. For example, the Services/Equipment/Transportation Committee is made up of three separate and functional subgroups — each with equal power and reporting to one working committee chairman. Alternatively, combine committees when necessary. Idle time and idle hands usually mean committee workers want to be better utilized.

When all positions are filled, complete the first full draft of the convention manual, showing everyone's position in the entire structure. Call a meeting of the executive and the working committee chairmen as soon as possible. Then arrange a follow-up meeting of the entire convention staff so everyone is aware of all current details. Continue the process at least once a month during final planning sessions.

How to run a meeting is the subject of many invaluable books and periodicals. Review this literature for the latest information. Set a time limit and agenda for every meeting, stick to essentials. Vitally important is a good committee secretary with the time and ability to move paper, keeping a record of all proceedings. Normally, the secretary resides in the same community as the chairman and co-chairman.

Secretaries must be excellent at organizing communication links, especially if working committees are scattered across the continent. Conference chairmen often complain about the difficulty in keeping their committees continually involved. Committee workers have the same complaints. They like to be active and aware of the conference chairman's latest thoughts and ideas. The process is accomplished through reports or assignments, issued through the secretary, on an immediate-action basis.

---

## EXECUTIVE COMMITTEE CHECKLIST

Develop Preliminary Conference Program ☐
Determine Conference Committee Structure ☐
Detail Committee Responsibilities ☐
Executive Committee Approval ☐
Select Committee Chairmen ☐
Select Committee Members ☐
Develop Preliminary Conference Budget ☐
Produce Convention Manual ☐

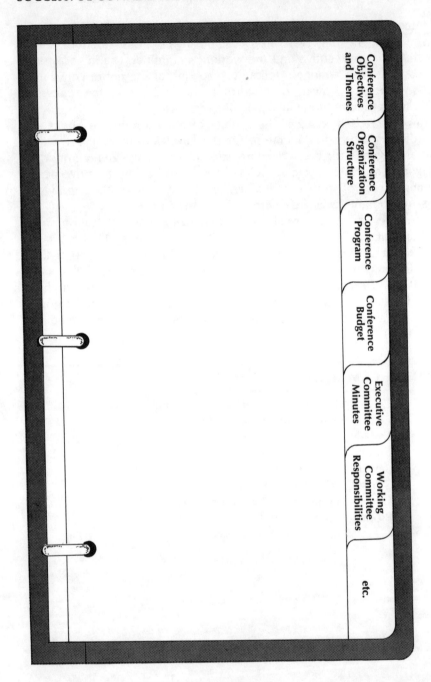

This sample convention manual is designed to ensure all working papers for all Executive and Committee Chairmen are kept in one place in an orderly fashion. All Committee members need their own manual.

Avoid Early
# COMMON PITFALLS

I t is easy for first-time convention planners to avoid conference chaos simply by remembering that eleven months' lead time is sufficient to effectively handle all convention details. Even the professional organizer will need this amount of time if prominent speakers must be recruited and major sponsors and exhibitors are required.

Eleven months means committees have sufficient time to make things happen. And from the beginning the conference chairman must see to it that each committee is actively working at its assignments. Taking this for granted could be a major error of judgment. Because working committee tasks are minimal at the initial stages you could find them postponing action.

Right now the conference chairman and the executive committee want to have data essential to all remaining conference planning. Each committee should complete, within one month, task sheets for the following:

Program session and event proposals
Estimates of revenue and expense
Responsibilities
Deadline guides

It's good policy for each working committee to evaluate the preliminary program as soon as possible. Break down each session and event into more concrete details, showing how they can be handled better. Very quickly you will be able to determine which of the many detailed proposals will be successful, which need revision, and indeed those which are best eliminated. It's wise to assume that unless a proposed session or event is a crowd pleaser, delegate attendance will probably be less than that achieved at the organization's previous conference.

Budgeting early sets every program proposal in proper perspective. It's a sound policy to estimate revenues low and expenses high. This builds in buffers which will probably evaporate with time but it postpones fund overruns. In any event, every program idea and its accoutrements cost money. The sooner working committees find sponsors or alternate income sources to minimize the strain on general conference coffers, the better.

Material and equipment requirements of each committee are financial facts of life. Services/Equipment/Transportation Committees obtain cost estimates for working committees. Actual committee and delegate needs must come from consultation with the working committees themselves.

Detailing these assignments on task sheets is quite straightforward. They consist of all duties during the next eleven months, as well as during and after the conference.

That nothing in life gets done on its own is a truism of every conference and convention task. It means listing tasks that must be performed by other committees in support of every individual committee. The Family Committee, for example, may require children's hats. Other committees in turn are responsible for purchase, design and supply. Finance must know the hats are within the budget. Services must deliver them to the Family Committee. Coordinating the entire detail is the key factor.

Task sheets should be used as reminders to get things done. That is why responsibilities and deadlines are so essential to good conference planning. Task cut-off dates become actual objectives, rather than tasks themselves. Deadlines provide goals and dates so jobs can be spaced out over several months. Why and when do events have to occur? How many can be achieved right away?

Expect task sheets from the Speakers' Committee, for example, to be along the following lines:

---

### I PROGRAM: (SPEAKERS' COMMITTEE)

---

Four Breakfast Sessions: One welcome speech and one farewell speech by conference chairman. Three breakfast chairmen.

Three Luncheon Sessions: One welcome speech by association past president. One welcome speech by major local official. One comedy speech. Three luncheon chairmen.

Three Dinner Sessions: One theme development speech by major international speaker. One "eye on the future" speech by major international speaker. One "state of the union" speech by incoming association president. Three dinner chairmen.

First Work Session: Concurrent sessions, four speakers, four session chairmen.

Second Work Session: Open session with one speaker and four panelists, one session chairman.

Annual Meeting: Open session with association past president as chairman.

Third Work Session: Concurrent sessions, four industry representatives and supporting experts, four session chairmen.

## II BUDGET:

### Expenses

Breakfast: Speakers' Travel: .................... $———————
Speakers' Accommodation: ........... $———————
Speakers' Fees: .................... $———————
Chairmen's Expenses, Equipment,
Hosting, etc: .................... $———————

Luncheon: Speakers' Travel: .................... $———————
Speakers' Accommodation: ........... $———————
Speakers' Fees: .................... $———————
Chairmen's Expenses, Equipment,
Receptions, etc: .................. $———————

Dinner: Speakers' Travel: .................... $———————
Speakers' Accommodation: ........... $———————
Speakers' Fees: .................... $———————
Chairmen's Expenses, Equipment,
Receptions, etc: .................. $———————

First Work Session:
Speakers' Travel: .................... $———————
Speakers' Accommodation: ........... $———————
Speakers' Fees: .................... $———————
Chairmen's Expenses, Equipment,
Hosting: ....................... $———————
Room Rental .................. $——————— $———————

Second Work Session:
Speakers' Travel: .................... $———————
Speakers' Accommodation: ........... $———————

Speakers' Fees: ..................... $_____

Panelists' Travel: ..................... $_____

Panelists' Accommodation: ........... $_____

Panelists' Fees: ..................... $_____

Chairmen's Expenses, Equipment,
    Hosting: ......................... $_____
        Room Rental ................... $_____   $_____

**Annual Meeting:**
    President/Chairman Expenses
        Equipment: ...................... $_____
        Room Rental ................... $_____   $_____

**Third Work Session:**
    Representatives' Travel: .............. $_____
    Representatives' Accommodation: ..... $_____
    Representatives' Fees: ................ $_____
    Consultants' Travel: ................. $_____
    Consultants' Accommodation: ........ $_____
    Consultants' Fees: ................... $_____
    Chairmen's Expenses
        Equipment, Hosting: .............. $_____
        Room Rental ................... $_____   $_____

**Additional Expenses:**
    Speakers' Suite: ..................... $_____
    Speakers' Reception Suite: ............ $_____
    Major Speakers' Gifts: ............... $_____
    Session Speakers' Gifts: .............. $_____
    Panelists' Gifts: ..................... $_____
    Representatives' Gifts: ............... $_____
    Consultants' Gifts: .................. $_____   $_____
                                        TOTAL $_____

**Revenues:**
    Complimentary Air Travel Allowances -
        Five Speakers: ................... $_____
    Travel Paid by Speakers: ............. $_____
    Travel Paid by Industry, etc: ......... $_____
    Complimentary Hotel Accommodation
        Allowance - One Speaker Per Night: . $_____
    Accommodation Paid by Speaker: ..... $_____
    Accommodation Paid by Industry, etc: . $_____
    Fees Waived by Speakers: ........... $_____
    Sponsored Reception Suite: .......... $_____   $_____
                                        TOTAL $_____

    Overrun from General Funds (if
        applicable) ...................... $_____

## III MATERIAL AND EQUIPMENT REQUIREMENTS:

- 1 Speakers' Reception Suite
- 3 Speakers' Suites (1 Night Each)
- 5 Panelists' Rooms (Single, 1 Night Each)
- 3 Speakers' Rooms (Single, 1 Night Each)
- 4 50-Seat Meeting Rooms (Concurrent Sessions)
- 4 100-Seat Meeting Rooms (Annual Meeting)
- 8 Movie Projectors
- 8 Movie Screens
- 1 Total, Transportable Sound System with 6 Panel Mikes and 6 Floor Mikes (Maximum Requirement)
- 7 Major Speakers' Gifts
- 10 Session Speakers' Gifts
- 8 Panelists' and Consultants' Gifts
- Refreshments
- Conference Letterhead
- Envelopes
- 1 Photocopier (Rental)
- Typewriters, Paper, Pencils, etc.

## IV RESPONSIBILITIES:

Selection of Session and Speaker Topics
List Major Speakers, Session Speakers and Panelists
Develop Presentation Method for Each Session
Estimate Attendance for Each Session
Coordinate Room Selection with Accommodation Committee
Provide Advance Information to Program Committee
Invite Major Speakers, Session Speakers and Panelists
Confirm Acceptances, Invite Alternates
Provide Final Information to Program Committee
Obtain Speakers' Travel, Accommodation, Indemnity, and Equipment Requirements
Obtain Speakers' Biographies
Provide Biographic Information to Media and Program Committees
Request Travel, Accommodation and Equipment from Relevant Committees
Select, Obtain Gifts for All Speakers and Panelists
Invite Session Chairmen as Necessary
Confirm Acceptances, Invite Alternates
Convene Session Chairmens' Meeting
Pickup and Hosting of Major Speakers, Session Speakers and Panelists
Receptions, Major Speakers
Presentation Speakers and Panelists' Gifts
Remittance Speakers, Panelists' Indemnities
Thank You Letters to All Speakers, Panelists, Chairmen, Sponsors
Obtain Copies All Speeches

Check to Prevent Overlapping Material
Distribute Speeches to Media Committee
Prepare Evaluation Questionnaires
Remit Questionnaires to Post-Conference Committee
Representation on Post-Conference Committee

## V DEADLINES:

Expand the responsibilities sheet and arrange the workloads on five charts as follows:

- MONTHS TO CONVENTION
  11, 10, 9, 8, 7, 6, 5, 4, 3, 2
- WEEKS TO CONVENTION
  4, 3, 2
- DAYS TO CONVENTION
  7, 6, 5, 4, 3, 2, 1
- CONVENTION ACTION DAYS
  1, 2, 3, 4
- POST-CONVENTION WEEKS
  1, 2, 3, 4

Each working committee should understand that task sheets developed eleven months before the conference can hardly be called final papers. Actually, they are only useful to set each task and deadline on paper for executive committee review. Each task and deadline will be modified as more facts become known. Each task sheet will change significantly as each committee incorporates the needs of the other committees. In fact, all task sheets once completed, will be modified into individual event schedules for every conference happening. At that point, the task sheets will no longer be needed. In Chapter 26 these typical event schedules are discussed in detail.

In the interim, work on the five task sheets must go ahead. Each committee has 30 days — no more. In the process, you can see your committees in action for the first time and evaluate their strengths and weaknesses.

Watch for individuals who can be better utilized. Take into consideration their business experiences, their interests, their hobbies. Shift them to positions tailor-made for their talents and specialties. For instance, a choir leader, if you have one in your organization, might make an excellent entertainment chairman.

You will probably have to lend a hand at working committee meetings as well. Resist the temptation to take personal charge. Suggest to your working committee chairmen that basic meeting procedures usually result in meaningful planning.

Have an explicit reason for each meeting.
Select time and location convenient to all members.
Mail out agendas two weeks ahead, listing all discussion items.
Telephone follow-up 24 hours before the session.
Start the meeting on time, stating problems to be discussed.
Control discussions and call on everyone for solutions.
Get commitments from each committee member.
Adjourn the meeting on time.

It is readily apparent then that month eleven is perhaps the most crucial in the conference process. Expenses, revenues, program, equipment, services and personnel have to be identified. Whatever you do, do it early. This is the real secret to avoiding conference pitfalls.

## THE CONFERENCE TIMETABLE

**Eleven Months To Convention:**

Prepare Committee Task Sheets ☐
Develop Main Conference Budget ☐
Update Conference Manuals ☐
Convene Executive Committee Meeting ☐
Convene Program Meeting — All Committees ☐

**Ten Months To Convention:**

Develop Program Sessions and Events ☐
Initiate Speaker Recruitment ☐
Initiate Sponsor Solicitation ☐
Initiate Exhibit Solicitation ☐
Determine Room Charges ☐
Negotiate Hotel Meeting Rooms ☐
Develop Advance Program ☐
Determine Delegate Fees and Expenses ☐
Complete Main Conference Budget ☐
Complete Accounting, Auditing and Banking Procedures ☐

**Nine Months To Convention:**

Continue Speaker Recruitment ☐
Initiate Panelist Recruitment ☐
Initiate Moderator Recruitment ☐
Continue Sponsor Solicitation ☐
Continue Exhibit Solicitation ☐
Develop Advance Program ☐
First News Release ☐
First Delegate Bulletin ☐
Develop Pre-Registration Procedures ☐
Print Delegate Registration Forms ☐
Acquire Conference Hotel Registration Forms ☐

**Eight Months To Convention:**

Complete Program Sessions and Events ☐
Complete Speaker Recruitment ☐
Continue Panelist Recruitment ☐
Continue Moderator Recruitment ☐
Second Delegate Bulletin ☐
Distribute Preliminary Program ☐
Distribute Registration Forms ☐
Distribute Accommodation Forms ☐
Continue Sponsor Solicitation ☐
Continue Exhibitor Solicitation ☐
Prepare Internal Forms and Records ☐
Print Event Tickets ☐

**Seven Months To Convention:**

Complete Speaker Arrangements ☐
Complete Panelist Recruitment ☐
Complete Moderator Recruitment ☐
Second News Release ☐
Third Delegate Bulletin ☐
Initiate Pre-Registration Process ☐
Confirm Meeting Room Requirements ☐
Confirm Convention Menus ☐
Prepare Conference Tender Documents ☐
Distribute Conference Tender Forms to Suppliers ☐
Continue Sponsor Solicitation ☐
Continue Exhibitor Solicitation ☐

**Six Months To Convention:**

Complete Panelist Arrangements ☐
Complete Moderator Arrangements ☐
Fourth Delegate Bulletin ☐
Continue Pre-Registration Process ☐
Acquire Local Attractions Literature ☐
Acquire Tourist Literature ☐
Complete Security Arrangements ☐
Complete Insurance Arrangements ☐

**Five Months To Convention:**

Continue Sponsor Solicitation ☐
Develop Meeting Room Layouts ☐
Develop Dining Room Layouts ☐
Complete Tender Calls For Materials and Supplies ☐
Continue Pre-Registration Process ☐
Continue Exhibitor Solicitation ☐

**Four Months To Convention:**

Continue Sponsor Solicitation ☐
Complete Exhibitor Solicitation ☐
Distribute Exhibitor Contracts ☐
Complete All Materials, Supplies, Arrangements ☐
Complete Meeting Room Layouts ☐
Complete Dining Room Layouts ☐
Complete Pre-Registration Process ☐
Mail Hotel Accommodation Acceptance Forms ☐
Confirm Attendance to Hotel ☐

**Three Months To Convention:**

Continue Sponsor Solicitation ☐
Complete Exhibitor Arrangements ☐
Prepare Final Program ☐
Final Program Meeting — All Committees ☐
Final Planning Report ☐
Confirm Meeting Room Layouts with Hotel ☐
Confirm Dining Room Layouts with Hotel ☐

**Two Months To Convention:**

Print Formal Program ☐
Contact Local and National Media ☐
Hire All Outside Staff ☐
Prepare Conference Evaluation Questionnaires ☐
Distribute Detailed Speakers' Instructions ☐
Confirm Menus, Refreshments with Hotel ☐

**Four Weeks To Convention:**

Mail Formal Program To Delegates ☐
Train Hosting Staff ☐
Arrange for Advertising Copy ☐

**Three Weeks To Convention:**

Complete Media Room Layout ☐
Train Registration Staff ☐

**Two Weeks To Convention:**

Complete Media Requirements ☐
Train Media Staff ☐
Begin Daily Monitoring of Conference Deliveries to Hotel ☐

**Seven Days To Convention:**

Trial Run with Hotel Staff ☐

**Six Days — Five Days — Four Days To Convention:**

    Begin Filling Delegates' Kits ☐

    Complete Filling Delegates' Kits ☐

    Distribute Kits to Local Delegates ☐

**Three Days To Convention:**

    Advertising Commences ☐

**Two Days To Convention:**

    Event Rehearsals ☐

    Open Conference Office ☐

**One Day To Convention:**

    Open Registration Center ☐

    Open Media Center ☐

    Open Hospitality Center ☐

    Set Up Exhibits ☐

    Conference Staff Moves into Hotel ☐

**Convention Action Day One:**

    Pre-Function Check: Every Event ☐

    Opening News Conference ☐

    Attendance Audit — Confirm with Hotel ☐

    Complete Exhibits Area ☐

    Open Exhibits Area ☐

**Convention Action Days Two, Three And Four:**

    Check Speakers' Schedule ☐

    Check News Conference Schedules ☐

    Solve Previous Day's Problems and Avoid Recurrences ☐

    Pre-Function Check: Every Event ☐

    Attendance Audit — Confirm with Hotel ☐

**Post-Convention Week One:**

    Transcription of Proceedings ☐

    Preparation of Thank You Letters ☐

    Payment of Conference Accounts ☐

    Distribution Conference Evaluation Questionnaires ☐

**Post-Convention Week Two:**

    Edit Conference Proceedings ☐

    Payment of Conference Accounts ☐

    Mail Conference Thank You Letters ☐

**Post-Convention Week Three:**

    Print Conference Proceedings ☐

    Audit of Conference Revenues and Expenditures ☐

**Post-Convention Week Four:**

       Payment of Outstanding Conference Accounts ☐

       Distribute Conference Proceedings ☐

       Print Conference Audited Statement ☐

       Distribute Conference Audited Statement ☐

       Tabulate Conference Evaluation Questionnaires ☐

       Prepare Conference Evaluation Report ☐

       Distribute Conference Evaluation Report ☐

# 9

## Knowing About
# THE DELEGATES

**U**nderstanding your delegates and generating involvement is vital no matter what type of conference or convention is under consideration. Delegates are individuals with differences which you cannot afford to ignore.

Generally speaking, delegate motivation falls into three broad categories. These motivations can cause pleasure or heartache, in direct relation to the scope and emphasis of your conference program. This consideration must be an integral part of your conference planning.

Category one includes delegates who must attend. Perhaps their employers demand participation. More likely still is a desire to attend the conference because of nomination or election, or because the gathering is critical to the delegate's professional role.

Category two represents those delegates who should attend. The conference functions to fulfill staff training needs or some other company or personal objective. Additionally, the conference will provide peer-relationships as well as an opportunity for individual participation.

Category three encompasses delegates who would like to attend. They are seeking three or four days away from the office, receiving an employer-sponsored benefit, or an opportunity to meet personal friends outside the convention.

Whatever the motivation, delegates consciously or subconsciously anticipate certain conference benefits. They require information on the conference at the earliest possible date so they know what will happen during the sessions. This implies that it is expected that all sessions are relevant to the purposes of the conference and will start and stop at predetermined times. Some will convene private meetings related to the topics of formal sessions. Attendees expect to participate fully as conference delegates. It is also an expected and essential right of each delegate to meet senior executives and as many other delegates and speakers as possible.

And all organization members as well as the delegates expect to receive conference papers, proceedings and evaluations immediately following the conclusion of the event.

It is only common courtesy to ensure equal and fair treatment of all delegates while they are in your care. Too often this is loosely interpreted to mean programs and hospitality kits, delegate identification, registration fee information and a room reservation form. It goes well beyond that.

The conference organization itself, not the hotel, is responsible for equitable room accommodation according to the hotel's posted schedule. The effective conference organization provides the full facilities of a convention information office, staffed with people who are responsive and capable of resolving delegate differences and needs.

While researching this area remember it is a wise policy to let your conference hotel management know the things which concern your delegates. Include items such as: late meals, and coffee breaks, dirty glasses and cutlery, understaffed cafeterias and front desks, room service delays and those other small irritations which can be avoided.

Moreover, every delegate has the right to detailed information on out-of-conference events, reputable restaurants and shopping outlets, state or provincial regulations, civic or municipal bylaws, hotel rates across the city and other relevant local information.

And, it goes without saying, delegates have to be told who pays for what and when it is to be paid. This also applies to every VIP, organization executive, speaker, panelist or committee member.

Where necessary, it is in your best delegate-planning interests to provide complete statements of Foreign Convention Attendance. For instance, Canada and the United States have corporate and personal income tax regulations pertaining to conferences which need to be monitored on a year-to-year basis.

Tax policies applicable to delegate travel, accommodation and session attendance at corporate expense have been in effect for several years. Special statements have not been required from conference organizers for these purposes. It is a different set of circumstances for delegates attending non-domestic meetings which are seen as personal junkets taken at the expense of taxpayers.

These laws then, usually apply to individuals attending your convention at their own expense. Surveys show that 83 per cent of all convention delegates are on company expense accounts. Your concern is with those who aren't. They will need the appropriate forms if they are attending your convention from outside the country.

If you are expecting American delegates at a Canadian convention write the Internal Revenue Service, Treasury Department, Washington D.C., 20224, for the latest regulations and current statement of Foreign Convention Attendance Forms. American convention organizers, on the other hand, should write Revenue Canada, Ottawa, Ontario for current brochures and forms.

Customs regulations are equally important to your foreign delegates. Canadian convention chairmen can obtain complete information from Canadian Customs, Connaught Building, MacKenzie Avenue, Ottawa, K1A 0L5, Canada. American chairmen should contact their nearest customs office for the appropriate details.

Delegate requirements and responsibilities such as these highlight the sensitive attention to detail which is required of each working committee. If every committee member understands these interrelated factors, then the stage is set for realistic convention planning.

In the delegate care sector, the Finance or Budget Committee is responsible for obtaining insurance to cover every eventuality, in addition to theft in the exhibit area. It means an all-inclusive policy that will compensate delegates, committee, organization, sponsors, exhibitors and other participants alike for public liability, fire, theft, loss of equipment or materials, food poisoning, medical assistance and accidents. Seek the advice of a reputable insurance agent on other possible requirements.

Seldom purchased but good insurance value is "tenants' fire legal liability" — a policy which protects delegates and the committee from damage claims instituted by the convention hotel as the result of careless incidents during the conference.

Costs vary for these special insurance policies. But uncovered claims are a different story. Beware — some hotels will suggest their own insurance policies cover most, if not all, situations. Have an insurance agent check the hotel's policies and get coverage to fill in the gaps. Experienced planners have been known to include convention cancellation coverage. This protects against revenue losses due to transportation or hotel strikes or other problems beyond the conference committee's control which cause the convention to be cancelled.

## DELEGATE-NEEDS CHECKLIST

Review Delegate Motivations ☐

Complete Delegate Profile ☐

Match Hotel Accommodation to Delegate Needs ☐

Match Events to Delegate Preferences ☐

Obtain Delegate Insurance Coverage ☐

Obtain Delegate Tax Brochures ☐

Plan for Maximum Delegate Involvement and Satisfaction ☐

# 10

Conference Financing –
## COST CONTROL HINTS

**F**irst thoughts, interim thoughts and final thoughts throughout every conference exercise must certainly be finances. Where are the convention funds coming from? How much? How soon? How can money make money? One way or another, money is needed to balance the invoices and bills that must inevitably be paid before you can say the conference is truly a success.

Simple accounting records work for 50-delegate conferences. However, organizers undertaking a series of events on behalf of any association can count on an audited statement being required. If you are convening a program on behalf of private industry, the company accountants will audit the books and records. But without doubt large and small conventions need an in-depth accounting system if any semblance of financial control is to be expected.

The only logical solution is to marry an auditor at the earliest possible moment, seek his or her advice, and set up an accounting system which will allow a professional examination of the expenses and revenues. You require an audit which shows everything in proper financial order.

Most conference experts suggest normal accounting procedures fall well short of controlling expenditures incurred by five or more committees. Perhaps the greatest financial fallout occurs when revenues are balanced against expenditures after all expenses and costs are in. There is an answer to this impasse. Drop the usual committee revenue and expense accounting procedures and replace them with a modern convention cost control technique. Most effective in the authors' experience is a system they have developed—individual event budget control.

Separate or individual event budgets show anticipated incomes and expenses for each and every convention happening. All event expenditures must be offset by revenues. Separate event budgets identify those which will be less than self-liquidating or will fail to realize a profit. Then they can be examined in a very cold light months before the convention.

In fact, separate event budgets are almost a necessity. Many committees incur expenses and receive no revenue, so committee budgets are a sad way to control costs. Furthermore, if you are seeking sponsors, they should be picking up the total event cost, not just a portion. That means seeking additional funds from other sources or sponsors.

The event budget technique means cost cross-links with every committee. It is up to the Finance Committee to ride herd on event expenditures and keep all committee chairmen in the money picture. Good Finance Committees have total supervision of the following areas: budget, control of funds, cheque cashing controls, credit controls, purchasing controls, accounting and records, security precautions, banking arrangements, payment of accounts and post-conference audit.

One secret of increased conference revenues is the philosophy of making money earn money by requesting early payment of registration fees, sponsorship donations and exhibit rental charges. The value of having $20,000 on hand and invested in a high-interest deposit is more than obvious. If that kind of money is on deposit for six months, the conference chairman can schedule one or two extra events at no cost to anyone.

Most Finance Committees need advance funds from the national or local organization to operate, pending receipt of conference revenues. A good working capital position can usually be established at four per cent of total proposed conference expenses. Keep as much of these funds as possible in an interest-earning bank account as well.

The budget will probably shape up in the following manner:

## CONFERENCE BUDGET

RECEIPTS:
    Registration: 300 Members @ ......... $_____
             100 Spouses ............. $_____

100 Children ............ $————

Miscellaneous Event Tickets .......... $————

Exhibit Rentals ..................... $————

Sponsorships ...................... $————

Donations ......................... $————

National Advances ................. $————

Local Advances ................... $———— $————

DISBURSEMENTS:

Major Events (Per Schedule) .......... $————

Awards, Gifts ...................... $————

Speakers .......................... $————

Displays (Promotion, Rental) .......... $————

Printing, Postage (Pre-Convention) ..... $————

Registration, Media, Duplicating ....... $————

Services, Transportation, Equipment .... $————

Sound Rentals, Telephone, Telex ...... $————

Conference Committee Accommodation $————

Miscellaneous (Audit, Complimentaries) . $————

National Rebates ................... $————

Local Rebates ..................... $———— $————

Anticipated Surplus ................. $————

## SCHEDULE: MAJOR SESSIONS AND EVENTS

TUESDAY/9:00 a.m. - 5:00 p.m. - *Executive Council Session*

REVENUES:

Receipts ........................... $————

Sponsorships ....................... $————

Donations (Paper, Pencils, Flowers) .... $———— $————

DISBURSEMENTS:

Room Rental ...................... $————

Sound System Rentals ............... $————

Movie Equipment Rentals ........... $————

Photography ....................... $————

Stationery, Supplies ............... $————

Flowers .......................... $———— $————

SURPLUS/DEFICIT ............... $————

TUESDAY/7:00 p.m. - 9:00 p.m. - *Registration*

REVENUES:

Receipts .......................... $————

Sponsorships (Travel Agency) ......... $————

Donations (Typewriters, Programs,

Briefcases, Miscellaneous Gifts) ...... $———— $————

DISBURSEMENTS:

Space Rental ........................ $——————

Equipment Rentals ................. $——————

Delegates Kits ...................... $——————

Staff Salaries ....................... $——————

Stationery, Supplies ................. $—————— $——————

SURPLUS/DEFICIT ................. $——————

TUESDAY/7:00 p.m. - 9:00 p.m. - *Reception*

REVENUES:

Receipts (Ticket Sales) .............. $——————

Sponsorships (Major Industry) ........ $——————

Donations (Distillery, Food Processor,

Manufacturer) .................... $—————— $——————

DISBURSEMENTS:

Space Rental ........................ $——————

Sound Equipment Rentals ............. $——————

Entertainment ...................... $——————

Food ............................... $——————

Refreshments ...................... $——————

Corkage ........................... $——————

Tip ............................... $——————

Gifts ............................. $——————

Miscellaneous (Supplies) .............. $—————— $——————

SURPLUS/DEFICIT ................. $——————

Note several important items. All miscellaneous items should contain a contingency allowance. Maintaining a firm budget means written, detailed bids from convention hotels, suppliers and consultants. Where prices cannot be obtained for events, services and goods well in advance, obtain notice of when final prices will be available. They should be prices geared to the cost of living. Generally speaking, prices should be confirmed six months before the convention begins.

Place a dollar value on all material donations to ensure total cost control. Debit and credit donations as though they involved revenues and expenditures.

It bears repeating: every event must have a separate budget account. As the months go by and funds are limited, separate event budgets show where funds may have to be restricted or more sponsors encouraged to take part. Each event may incur the following expenses—make certain they are considered before establishing actual costs:

☐ Conference materials

☐ Consultants' fees

☐ Equipment rentals

☐ Guards/Commissionaires

- ☐ Hotel Guarantees
- ☐ Insurance
- ☐ Overtime — casual staff
- ☐ Signs, prizes, flowers, gifts
- ☐ Speakers, travel, accommodation, fees, etc.
- ☐ Standby equipment
- ☐ Transportation

Financial control also means on-the-floor management during each convention event. Far too many conferences suffer financial reverses after the conference starts, not before. The best way to keep expenses in hand when the convention is in progress is to take head counts of delegates and others attending every event.

The conference hotel has a similar operating policy, particularly when food and beverages are being served. Count heads with a hotel employee before the function report is turned over to the hotel's accounting office. The Finance Committee must have full authority to sign all hotel function invoices—on the convention floor. There should be no tipping at this time. Gratuities are better calculated on all final hotel bills after discussion by the conference chairman and the Finance Committee.

Further financial savings can be effected by checking liquor laws and hotel refreshment policies. In certain provinces and states you can provide all refreshments and pay hotel corkage fees on a per-bottle basis. In any case, determine all bottle charge considerations. Some hotels charge solely on the number of drinks consumed. Others go on the basis of the number of empty and open bottles. Who gets the "heels" can be a problem—the responsibility of the Finance Committee.

Financial accountability can be assured by implementing an all-event ticket system. It means printing ticket books containing entry tickets for every event, regardless of type, cost or sponsorship. The advantages are many. This process controls outsiders, verifies head counts, shows hotel management the committee is running a business-like operation and keeps an unobtrusive yet effective financial control on all convention activities.

Additionally, event tickets can be used for session attendance promotion purposes. Once the event tickets are processed, they can go into a drum. Prize draws can then become a highlight of the farewell breakfast. If you are thinking in this vein, color-code tickets to identify delegates, spouses, children and committee workers. When the tickets have moved through the accounting process, discard, if you wish, the local committee ticket stubs. This system creates goodwill because the attendance prizes go to out-of-town visitors. Preferably you will avoid ticket draws at every session. Aside from detracting from the event's intended purpose, regular draws become monotonous.

Finally—it shouldn't have to be said—the Finance Committee must never accept an invoice unless the expenditure was previously budgeted. This procedure, made known to every committee in advance, is the only sure way to rein in and control expenses. A statement of this policy, together with revenue and expenditure sheets, should be distributed to all committees and included in the conference manuals.

## FINANCE COMMITTEE CHECKLIST

| | |
|---|:---:|
| Hire an independent auditor | ☐ |
| Establish budget priorities | ☐ |
| Prepare draft budget | ☐ |
| Determine conference accounting system | ☐ |
| Determine conference accounting forms | ☐ |
| Develop event budgets for each conference item | ☐ |
| Review costs from previous conferences | ☐ |
| Review draft budget with Executive Committee | ☐ |
| Review all draft tender and contract documents | ☐ |
| Acquire formal bids from all suppliers | ☐ |
| Acquire written agreements with hotel | ☐ |
| Select reputable suppliers, not necessarily lowest bidders | ☐ |
| Request early payment of sponsors' and exhibitors' payments and fees | ☐ |
| Request early payment of delegate fees | ☐ |
| Draft final budget | ☐ |
| Control all conference funds | ☐ |
| Control all conference credit and revenue | ☐ |
| Control banking and chequing arrangements | ☐ |
| Control committee expenditures | ☐ |
| Approve all expenditures before commitment | ☐ |
| Control safety and security precautions | ☐ |
| Control conference insurance requirements | ☐ |
| Control VIP and delegate credit limits | ☐ |
| Control all accounting and records | ☐ |
| Complete payment of accounts | ☐ |
| Complete post-conference audit | ☐ |

# 11

## Successful Techniques of
## SPONSOR SALESMANSHIP

**T**he most demanding conference responsibility is the work of the Sponsor Committee. Its job is to seek sponsorships and donations of goods, services and equipment, plus the solicitation of everything and anything which will help balance the convention books. Of course, these donations should only be sought if they are acceptable to your organization.

Make no mistake, this is a job for committee members with sound business, industry, education and professional connections. The chairman of this committee needs these attributes many times over, and they are prerequisites for every Sponsor Committee member.

Unless the conference is to be underwritten entirely by one organization, obtaining sponsorships and donations means long hours of solid digging. The technique here is to use every possible personal contact. In fact, the responsibility extends throughout the entire association on a national, and perhaps, international basis. A major speaker who does not require expenses or fees could save the convention $1,000 or more. Opportunities like this cannot be overlooked. It simply means having the right member making the initial personal contact.

Remember too, that local, state or provincial and federal governments will often provide funds, speakers and services. It's donations of people, time, services and supplies which dramatically cut convention costs.

Sponsor solicitation is seldom an easy task, even with all the committee members and delegates on the lookout for convention dollars and services. Some 9,000 international and national conventions of one kind or another are under way every year. Your Sponsor Committee is in daily competition with other convention organizers and there are only so many sponsor dollars to go around. Obviously, there are not enough funds available to satisfy every convention each year.

So sponsorship solicitation becomes a science, not a game. What is the key to successful solicitation? All sponsors have the same goal. They expect to receive fair value in keeping with their own goals commensurate with their conference investment—this is their true measurement device. It applies to every sponsor without exception—government, education, industry, professional organizations, foundations or private enterprise.

Unless a committee member can present valid reasons for a potential sponsor's participation in the conference, you know what the sponsor's answer will be before the question is asked. All prospective sponsors expect a detailed and informative outline of the conference objectives, themes, speakers, delegate profiles, and, most essential, the draft program.

Stress display exposure for exhibit sponsors and community and corporate benefits for event sponsors. Few prospective sponsors get this type of information. Even more rare is the occasion when a sponsor receives a detailed description of a particular event which means profit and ideal exposure.

State clearly and precisely those advantages of real value to the potential sponsor. After all, most sponsors receive countless proposals every year. They are well accustomed to solicitation techniques. This is why Sponsors Committees need an effective presentation which is in keeping with good business practice.

Nevertheless, sponsorship opportunities are almost unlimited. They include grants for entire conferences; delegate travel and conference expenses; speaker travel and expenses; youth sponsorships; space rentals; event sponsorships; session grants and operational costs. They also cover partial contributions for speakers, printed matter, meals, local transportation, hospitality suites and receptions.

Some donations are often overlooked because of their relatively low dollar value. Be prepared for a surprise. Often donations of equipment and services mean major savings. Donations range from the ridiculous to the sublime, yet each means reduced conference expenditures. Consider slides, films, printed matter, duplicating or copying equipment, typewriters, communications systems, audiovisual equipment, confer·

ence briefcases, memo pads, pens, pencils, paper, gifts, prizes, flowers, refreshments and products of all types. Above all realize that donations of speakers' time and talent, as well as loaned staff and executives, cut conference costs.

Major sponsorships give outside organizations the opportunity to mount a complete event, including providing speakers and a meal. Quite often, receptions and hospitality suites are classed in this category —a chance for sponsors to have a captive audience. Keep in mind though, their purposes must also be those of the convention itself.

Cash contributions with no strings attached, are undoubtedly the best for conference planning purposes. Of course a Sponsors Committee could hardly expect to use funds from a distillery to underwrite a beer and pretzel event. Care must also be taken to ensure that the sponsors' contribution is reflected in the conference itself. Major sponsors, for example, would be associated with the most important conference events.

If a sponsor can only undertake half the cost of an event, perhaps equal billing can be shared with another, non-competitive sponsor. Alternatively, if a total-event sponsor is found the money for a partially-sponsored event can be more effectively used elsewhere on the program.

A recent trend has been for some sponsors to insist on full credit although they are underwriting only 20 to 50 per cent of the cost of an event. If this is unsatisfactory and you are unable to compromise with a co-sponsor, then turn to a new sponsor as quickly as possible.

Private receptions and hospitality suites are passé at some conferences today, unless they are open to everyone. Instead schedule all-delegate receptions collectively sponsored by all erstwhile hospitality suite operators. In short, evolve a sponsor policy for control and avoid private, late-night parties.

In addition, the Sponsor Committee should have a public relations policy for its benefactors. Every sponsor should be invited to one special event. One good approach is opening the get-acquainted reception to all conference supporters and contributors.

Be realistic. Sponsors must get full credit on the conference program distributed to delegates if it is their wish. List sponsors on a separate program page, rather than in connection with a particular event. Invite dinner-event sponsor representatives to sit at head tables. They are acknowledged by the dinner chairman but no sponsor speech is necessary. Reception sponsors are introduced from the floor. Again, speeches are not required for the delegates or sought by responsible sponsors. Session sponsors are also acknowledged by the chairman, but refrain from delivering greetings or remarks unless they are a formal part of the session program.

The real secret of sponsor/donor solicitations is to make formal presentations to selected prospects at least one month before the sponsor's annual budget deadlines. In certain instances this means talking to sponsors 10 or 11 months before the convention begins. The idea is to obtain sponsorship agreements, free of budget restrictions, at an early stage when there is little competition from other conference organizers.

A basic accounting control is all that is needed by any Sponsor Committee. Three sub-accounts: 1) *Sponsorships Received*; 2) *Sponsorships Confirmed* and 3) *Sponsorships in Negotiation* will do the trick. But, if solicitations aren't going well, plan an intensive, last-minute campaign to encourage sponsorship participation. Quite often small donations will be forthcoming from those who could not earlier afford a significant contribution.

A few words here from sadder but wiser conference planners. Charges of influence peddling can emanate from the public and your delegates if donations appear to have been unjustly obtained, or, if sponsors seek to obtain favourable relationships. Such allegations have occurred at political conventions but can arise in any conference situation. Sponsor Committees be wary. Stay out of the sponsor area if something might go wrong.

If the decision is to solicit funds and services, then remember donations are only secure when they are deposited in the bank. Even formal confirmation letters are no guarantee in the event of business failure, change in government or in fluctuating economic situations.

Tie up contributions early and get them into the convention bank account. A sponsor in the bank is worth two in the bush.

---

## SPONSOR COMMITTEE CHECKLIST

| | |
|---|---|
| Draft a sponsor policy | ☐ |
| Review with Executive Committee | ☐ |
| Complete sponsor policy | ☐ |
| Set the sponsorship dollar goal | ☐ |
| List potential sponsors | ☐ |
| Encourage sponsors to underwrite total events cost | ☐ |
| Everyone is a Sponsor Committee member | ☐ |
| Contact sponsors during their budget preparation period | ☐ |
| Speakers and panelists could be sponsors | ☐ |
| Match potential conference events to potential sponsors | ☐ |
| Prepare sponsor solicitation packages | ☐ |
| Acknowledge sponsorships immediately | ☐ |
| Invite sponsors to pre-conference event | ☐ |
| Pass names of all sponsors to Printing Committee | ☐ |
| Continue to solicit sponsors until conference begins | ☐ |

Coordinate with Finance Committee     ☐

Prepare Conference Chairman's thank-you letters to
all sponsors     ☐

# 12

## The Current Scene in
# EXHIBITS AND DISPLAYS

**W**ould you believe a $2.5-million drilling rig, occupying more than an acre of exhibit space set up at a major convention? It was accomplished with 100 men and 50 trucks driven some 200 miles; put on for a national petroleum show, it attracted more than 40,000 viewers in addition to 18,000 registered delegates.

Yet, an increasing number of conferences, congresses and conventions are abandoning the business of exhibits and displays. Severe exhibit limitations confront many organizations—show space is non-existent or at best consists of an old, unheated hall. Few hotels, except those with the most modern convention facilities, have significant exhibit hall capabilities.

And not to be unremarked is the growing evidence of empty exhibit and display halls reflecting poor exhibitor response to conference overtures. Fewer consultants now involve themselves in exhibit promotion. The commissions they require often mean operating exhibit areas at a loss.

Why then are there still several experts in this field who continue to mount fascinating, high-profit exhibit programs year after year? Primarily, they are professionals with total-capability display houses—geared to submit comprehensive proposals, design suggestions and complete package estimates. They are the organizations which not only lay out the show but also build all the display booths that are required. Their services also include: installation of backdrops; booth renovations; erection, maintenance and dismantlement of displays as well as pre-show publicity. Basic costs for conference services by display houses usually are held to 15 per cent commissions. Their main income is derived from exhibit design, construction and maintenance on behalf of participating exhibitors.

Success essentials are easily identifiable. Every Exhibits Committee must offer exhibitors a totally professional program, backed up by a recognized display company. Sponsors have a right to know their involvement will pay dividends. Anything less and exhibitor interest is lost!

Line up potential sponsors before they complete the forthcoming year's budget for exhibits. The response then becomes: "Can we include the XYZ Convention in our commitments next year?" Not: "How do we find funds for XYZ's Convention next month?"

A good technique is suggesting to potential sponsors that the best exhibit they now have on hand, so long as it is related to the conference theme, is quite sufficient. If an exhibitor wants to allocate special funds for a new exhibit—well and good—but avoid this condition in conference promotional material as it will eliminate several exhibit sponsors.

Smart convention planners schedule a few major conference events right in the exhibit area. Receptions and some types of work sessions, for example, can be effectively staged within this setting. Obviously, exhibitors will be delighted that this is happening as it is a vital sponsor promotion and publicity opportunity. Suddenly the exhibit area becomes a prestige conference program locale.

Standard exhibit spaces are 10 feet x 10 feet across North America. Ready-made units on hand in most exhibitor's warehouses conform to this size standard, coming in single and multiple 10-foot lengths.

Insist on the standard size booth area at your conference. Some hotels will suggest sizes better related to their exhibit areas, perhaps 7 foot x 7 foot units, so it looks like double the number of booths. Forget it. Few exhibitors are prepared to cut up 10 foot x 10 foot units to fit 7 foot x 7 foot spaces. Redesign the exhibit hall layout to accommodate 10 foot x 10 foot units with 15 foot to 20 foot alleys. Tailor your booth rental rates accordingly.

Sponsors also expect media-promoted public viewing hours. Paid advertising, identifying all exhibitors and public viewing times, is the answer. Sales and marketing consultants, as well as advertising agencies, can help here. Don't overlook exhibit area entertainment during public viewing hours.

Exhibit security is a must. No exhibitor shows keen interest in conference committees which cannot protect exhibits, equipment and products from pilferage and damage. Hire security guards and institute round-the-clock surveillance for the duration of the convention.

The best bet is to develop a professional display contract between exhibitors, the hotel and the Exhibits Committee. Have the agreement checked by a local lawyer and the hotel's solicitors, then have it printed for distribution. The trick is to enclose three copies of the contract and the exhibit hall floor plan with every solicitation letter sent to prospective exhibitors. This will indicate that the Commitee knows what it is doing and is running a business-like operation.

Remember the law of contract varies widely, particularly from nation to nation, but the sample Display Agreement will probably suit most purposes and create the desired favourable impression of your conference organization.

THE NORTH AMERICAN PROMOTIONS
ASSOCIATION ANNUAL CONVENTION
BENSON BAY HOTEL, LANDMARK

EXHIBIT HALL, SECOND FLOOR — JULY 8, 9, 10, 11

## EXHIBIT LOUNGE CONTRACT

THIS AGREEMENT made in triplicate this ........ day of .............. A.D. between the NORTH AMERICAN PROMOTIONS ASSOCIATION as the ASSO-CIATION and ......................................... as the LESSEE.

1. The ASSOCIATION hereby grants the LESSEE the privilege to use space provided in the EXHIBIT LOUNGE, Seventh Floor, Benson Hotel as shown on the plan attached, subject to the conditions laid down by the ASSOCIATION as attached to this contract; which conditions are part of this AGREEMENT between the LESSEE and the ASSOCIATION for the period from July 8 to July 11, inclusive.

2. All space is sold in 10 foot by 10 foot units at $500.00 per unit.

3. The LESSEE agrees to pay the ASSOCIATION the total space rental upon signing and delivering this contract to the ASSOCIATION.

4. Final allocation of space shall be at the discretion of the ASSOCIATION. If it is the decision of the ASSOCIATION that re-location of an exhibitor is necessary to provide a better balanced EXHIBIT LOUNGE, then in that event the LESSEE shall abide by the decision of the ASSOCIATION.

5. This contract is not subject to cancellation by the LESSEE, but in the event the LESSEE cannot mount a display in the EXHIBIT LOUNGE the LESSEE has the right to sublet its contracted space to a SUB-LESSEE approved by the ASSOCIATION, subject to all terms and conditions of this contract.

6. The LESSEE agrees to confine his exhibit to the following rental space or spaces.

_____

IN WITNESS WHEREOF the parties hereto have executed and delivered these presents, the day and year first mentioned above.

Approved this ...... day of ............    NORTH AMERICAN PROMOTIONS ASSOCIATION

Receipt of $............. acknowledged

_____
Exhibit Chairman

_____    _____
WITNESS                                              LESSEE

PRINT BELOW EXHIBITING FIRM'S NAME AND MAILING ADDRESS:

_____

_____

## IMPORTANT NOTICE

Mail immediately to EXHIBIT CHAIRMAN, PROMOTIONS ASSOCIATION, LANDMARK. Make all cheques payable to THE NORTH AMERICAN PROMOTIONS ASSOCIATION.

### TERMS AND CONDITIONS

1. The LESSEE agrees his exhibit and display staff will be conducted in a satisfactory manner and further agrees to abide by all TERMS and CONDITIONS prescribed by the ASSOCIATION. The EXHIBIT LOUNGE COMMITTEE will be authorized representatives of the ASSOCIATION.

2. The LESSEE shall be entitled to all EXHIBIT LOUNGE passes as required by the LESSEE from the ASSOCIATION. EXHIBIT LOUNGE passes will not entitle staff or guests to participate in all or any other Convention events scheduled by the ASSOCIATION.

3. All buildings, tents, awnings, enclosures and structures erected by the LESSEE must have prior approval of the ASSOCIATION.

4. All business conducted by the LESSEE shall be conducted in a quiet and orderly manner; the LESSEE shall keep his premises neat and clean and all rubbish, garbage, paper etc., shall be the responsibility of the LESSEE.

5. No promotional device or schemes involving prizes, gifts, privileges or awards determined as the result of any contest, or by chance, shall be undertaken by the LESSEE unless the ASSOCIATION has been notified in writing, before the opening date of the EXHIBIT LOUNGE, of its exact nature and the details of its operation.

6.  All booths, exhibits and displays are to be self-contained within the space or spaces assigned to the LESSEE and the LESSEE will confine his business and activities to this leased area. The space leased under this contract cannot be subleased or assigned to other parties without the expressed written consent of the ASSOCIATION.

7.  Provision of drapes, lighting, partitioning, carpets, etc., as well as shipping, erection, maintenance, dismantling, crating, uncrating and crate storage and all other affairs related to the LESSEE'S exhibit are the LESSEE'S sole responsibility.

8.  Authorized representatives of the ASSOCIATION shall have full access to the EXHIBIT LOUNGE premises of the LESSEE at any time.

9.  Nothing whatsoever of the LESSEE shall be posted or glued on, tacked or nailed or screwed to, or otherwise attached to any column, wall, window, floor, ceiling or other parts of the Benson Bay Hotel building or hotel furniture and equipment.

10.  The LESSEE is entitled to use mechanical equipment and sound amplification equipment on receipt of express written approval from the ASSOCIATION. If the operation of said or any equipment disturbs exhibitors, the ASSOCIATION or the guests of the Benson Bay Hotel, the LESSEE will discontinue the source of the annoyance, if so requested by the ASSOCIATION.

11.  The LESSEE shall have the full right to distribute public relations matter, advertising and/or promotional goods and materials within the confines of his rental space or spaces. All such matter, goods and materials require approval of the ASSOCIATION prior to the formal opening of the EXHIBIT LOUNGE.

12.  All EXHIBIT LOUNGE exhibits, displays and materials and goods essential to these exhibits and displays shall be delivered and INVOICED PREPAID to the LESSEE care of the EXHIBIT LOUNGE, SECOND FLOOR, BENSON BAY HOTEL, DICKSON AVENUE, LANDMARK, for DELIVERY ONLY July 7, 19—, Mailing simply to the Hotel will incur additional and separate moving charges to the LESSEE.

13.  PROMOTION DISPLAYS, SMITH AVENUE, LANDMARK has been appointed design consultant and display service representative to the EXHIBIT LOUNGE. A full range of display and exhibit services are available from PROMOTION at reasonable cost to the LESSEE. The ASSOCIATION and the BENSON BAY HOTEL are not a part of, nor responsible for these arrangements.

14.  LESSEES will conform to the following hours in the EXHIBIT LOUNGE and/ or any other hours as may subsequently be determined by the ASSOCIATION:

| Tuesday | 8:00 p.m. to 6:00 p.m. | Set up Exhibits |
|---|---|---|
| Wednesday | 8:00 am. to 10:00 a.m. | Set up Exhibits |
| | 11:30 a.m. to 5:00 p.m. | Convention Sessions |
| | 6:00 p.m. to 9:00 p.m. | Public Showings |
| | 9:00 p.m. to 11:00 p.m. | Convention Sessions |
| Thursday | 9:00 a.m. to 2:00 p.m. | Public Showings |
| | 2:00 p.m. to 5:00 p.m. | Convention Sessions |

|  |  |  |
|---|---|---|
|  | 6:00 p.m. to 9:00 p.m. | Public Showings |
|  | 9:00 p.m. to 11:00 p.m. | Convention Sessions |
| Friday | 9:00 a.m. to 2:00 p.m. | Public Showings |
|  | 2:00 p.m. to 8:00 p.m. | Dismantle Exhibits |

15.  The BENSON BAY HOTEL will provide general illumination and in addition will supply one general lighting power outlet for each 10 foot of space contracted by the LESSEE. If additional electric connections and currents are required, the LESSEE must notify the BENSON BAY HOTEL electrician and the LESSEE will be required to pay for this additional service.

16.  The BENSON BAY HOTEL will provide storage space in the hotel garage for crates and materials of the LESSEE. All such crates and materials must be moved and stored at the LESSEE'S expense.

17.  The ASSOCIATION reserves the right to cancel this contract without notice and refund any payments thereon, either for circumstances beyond the control of the ASSOCIATION or for actions due to the LESSEE. If cancelled, the amount of refund shall only be reduced pro rata on the basis of occupancy.

18.  The LESSEE accepts full responsibility for all liabilities for damages to persons or property, public or private, arising out of the LESSEE'S use and occupancy of the BENSON BAY HOTEL premises and understands and accepts that this contract shall not be construed or implied as a partnership, but only as a lease and privilege concession to be paid for on a rental basis.

19.  The ASSOCIATION will take reasonable precaution to ensure the safety of the LESSEE'S exhibits, goods, machines and materials during the conference, but the LESSEE himself must take the full risk of exhibiting them. Should any exhibit, goods, machines and materials or portion thereof be injured, lost, stolen or suffer damages from any cause whatsoever, the ASSOCIATION and/or the BENSON BAY HOTEL will not be liable, or make payment for the value thereof.

20.  Neither the ASSOCIATION, nor the BENSON BAY HOTEL, nor PROMOTION DISPLAY shall be held responsible for the safety of exhibits against theft, fire, accident or any destructive cause, nor for accidents to LESSEES, their agents or employees. If insurance is required by the LESSEE, it must be placed by the LESSEE and shall be paid by the said LESSEE.

Regardless of the size of the exhibit program, the typical Exhibit Committee has the following assignments to complete during the coming months:

## EXHIBIT COMMITTEE CHECKLIST

|  |  |
|---|---|
| Detail floor area, obstructions, floor load, ceiling heights, outlets, lighting, power supply, air conditioning, loading areas, storage areas, hotel restrictions and legal requirements | ☐ |
| Detail access to exhibit area | ☐ |
| Book exhibit hall space | ☐ |

Determine exhibit lounge hours ☐

Design floor plan (to scale) ☐

Determine rental rates and confirm with executive
committee ☐

Design promotional signs, booth identification ☐

Design exhibit hall decor ☐

Complete display consultant agreement ☐

Determine freight receiving times ☐

Identify hotel staff for receiving exhibits ☐

Determine policies and practices with executive committee ☐

Prepare exhibitors' contracts ☐

Prepare solicitation letter ☐

Distribute exhibitors' solicitation material ☐

Distribute exhibitors' contracts ☐

Receive exhibitors' contracts ☐

Follow up exhibitors' solicitation as required ☐

Arrange security staff with finance committee ☐

Arrange exhibitor accommodation with
accommodation committee ☐

Distribute exhibit questionnaires ☐

Receive exhibit questionnaires ☐

Prepare promotional material for promotion and
media committees ☐

Pass exhibitors' names to printing committee ☐

Provide one copy of each exhibitor's contract to hotel,
display company and to exhibitor ☐

Request lighting, PA systems, photographer, desks,
chairs, telephones, office equipment and other items
from appropriate committees ☐

Ensure exhibit area security in force at all times ☐

Dismantle exhibits at end of convention ☐

# 13

## The Potential of
# A POSITIVE
# PROGRAM PLAN

**B**y now opening day should be some 10 months away and research and preliminary proposals are beginning to have dimension and meaning. Revenues are becoming fact rather than promise, delegates' wants are clearly understood and conference themes and objectives are firmly established. Early go-getting committees—particularly Sponsors and Exhibits—are well under way, and Finance is already penny-pinching.

It's time then for detailed program planning. At long last all the suggestions, thoughts and pipe-dream proposals can be subjected to in-depth examination. All should be analyzed, some will have to be discarded. Now the time-consuming research process, sometimes covering unfruitful ground, will bring big dividends as all committees contribute comments which are molded into a basic program plan.

The trick is to muster proposals to paper and evolve a down-to-the-minute timing sequence that will guarantee conference success. Detailed planning is an exciting and interesting undertaking. Suddenly the pieces of the jigsaw puzzle fit as committees understand, perhaps for the first time, how closely their separate responsibilities are interlocked. No one committee can exist without the support of all the others. Overlapping confusion, the bugbear of all conferences, is swept aside in the process.

If a small conference is contemplated — one that has worked well in the past — the entire operation can be managed with a single Program Committee. The ground is even safer when previous conferences have, by tradition, been highly structured. No changes may be necessary at all.

Program Committee workloads in these situations are hardly onerous. It's simply a job involving preparation of work sessions, selecting speakers, reviewing award nominations and arranging the required number of banquets and receptions. Time will have to be set aside for one or two spouse and youth events. Knit all this together, reflecting objectives and themes, and the program takes shape.

However, experienced conference planners know "yesterday's conference" is just that in our automated, animated, audiovisual society. Some experts claim waning attendance at conventions stems largely from poor programming. Pause and take stock of your situation. Positive policy and program changes might mean success in a big way.

Is a new conference technique long overdue? Perhaps an entire series of technical innovations face your industry. If so, switch from the usual state-of-the-ship convention and plan a workshop conference. Has your organization divided itself into specialized groupings? Why not identify them that way and develop special interest or occupational group sessions with four or five simultaneous conference programs?

Time and time again delegate complaints focus on lack of audience participation in the conference proceedings. In fact, delegate apathy is more than noticeable in several North American associations which are so huge that they have abandoned all-delegate annual meetings. In some instances the annual meeting is open to voting delegates before the actual conference begins. It is a mystery that members, asked to pay annual dues and urged to go to annual conferences, have little or no voice where it really counts — on the conference floor.

Detailed examination of this situation emphasizes the need for a meaningful series of speakers and total-participation sessions. Otherwise, delegates will go AWOL — to out-of-conference events, and criticize the sessions in private conversations. It is a clear case of a major breakdown in overall planning.

No matter what type of session best suits the conference purpose, the prime aim of each must be education. Our rapidly changing society can often make facts and ideas relevant 10 months ago obsolete. Tighten up the progress gap with learning situations.

Education sessions work when delegate groups are small, when speakers are nationally or internationally recognized and when delegates can move from lecture to lecture. Small group events should rarely exceed

20 minutes. For larger delegate audiences a session of approximately an hour is the outside limit.

The best education programs are those chaired and delivered by members of your own organization who have recently received national or international recognition for their achievements. Delegates seldom look at trophies or plaques. But it is surprising how many people want to find out just what program in the past year was good enough to win competitions or awards.

In a different vein, protocol in your organization may demand that the incumbent president chair all meetings. That's fine if you believe in dictatorship, but not good for a democratic association. Presidents must personally meet as many delegates as possible. This can't be done when they are at head tables and at private executive council sessions throughout the conference. If it can be managed, limit the president's official functions to the annual meeting, the opening session and change-in-stewardship event.

Conference chairmen and co-chairmen should be seen and not heard. Keep their head table appearances to one major dinner each. Working committee chairmen are the real heroes. Reward them with head-table chairmanships or session moderator appointments. Committee staff will gain delegate recognition by being included in receiving lines.

Points such as these are just the tip of the iceberg. The need to concern yourself with 100 delegates and more can make the detailed planning so extensive the Program Chairman may collapse in confusion. In such situations the detailed planning should be handled by a Program Group consisting of several sub-committees, all with equal authority. Names and groupings may vary, but a recommended organization of the sub-committees would be as follows:

**Program Group**

- ☐ Awards Committee
- ☐ Events Committee
- ☐ Sessions Committee
- ☐ Speakers Committee
- ☐ Spouses Committee

If necessary other committees can be added to the Program Group. Additions, however, should be made with purposeful co-operation as the intent, not as a matter of politics or prestige. This circumvents the possibility of a dangerously overloaded committee and makes for a more efficient operation. Sub-committee chairmen should have equal authority to ensure a minimum of difficulty in developing final plans and carrying out assignments. Here again you are practicing the art of effective convention management.

# 14

How To Win Speakers and
## INFLUENCE DELEGATES

**R**ather obvious but well worth repeating, good speakers — delivering pertinent material — can emphasize conference objectives and themes with dramatic impact. If your speakers represent the best experts in their respective fields then it means instant delegate interest and maximum media coverage for your convention.

Unfortunately, the supply of inadequate speakers is more than plentiful and usually a lot less expensive. Some are so compelled to speak, even about nothing, that they will pay for the opportunity to exhort anyone's delegates. This is not done openly of course. What happens is more sophisticated than that: "Mr. Ransom would be only too willing to finance a dinner, or a reception, if he learned the Speakers Committee wanted him to address the delegates." There is a saying that those who pay nothing for speakers get zero in the convention game.

If topics are to reflect conference objectives determined by the Executive Committee the potential speakers and panelists are quickly limited. Most Speakers Committees turn to experts, professionals or association executives in specialty subject areas for suggestions and ideas. They also obtain speakers' bureau listings prepared by business, sports organizations, industry, associations and foundations. The American Society of Association Executives, Canadian Boards of Trade, Chambers of Commerce, the Red Cross, the United Way and most federal, state, provincial and local governments maintain extensive speakers' lists.

Another reliable source of speakers is publishing houses, particularly those specializing in non-fiction. Universities are a literal and literate gold mine of speakers, most of whom are experienced public speakers after years of teaching. Keep in mind however that most authors and teachers depend upon writing or teaching, not speaking, for their financial success and reputation. A great authority who fails to communicate to your audience will be a poor choice whatever his or her educational background.

Speakers Committees seeking immediacy and relevancy to the conference program watch national news television programs and read pertinent publications. In the United States check *Business Week, Fortune, Meetings and Conventions, Newsweek, Successful Meetings, U.S. News & World Report* and *Time* magazines. *Macleans, Chatelaine, Comment, Saturday Night, The Financial Post,* and *Financial Times* are good Canadian sources. It is also worth checking the business press publications of Maclean-Hunter and Southam.

It is a fact that award winners within your own organization, particularly those recognized by other associations, are popular and elicit delegate interest. Consult the Awards Committee for recommendations.

Where the suggestions for speakers come from is not really important but don't take anyone's impressions and opinions for granted. The Speakers Committee must make telephone contacts and personal visits as mandatory tasks in assessing all speakers and panelists.

Articulate speakers are in constant demand. Topnotch men and women on the international circuit are often booked 18 or 20 months ahead. Nationally-recognized personalities are usually available 8 to 10 months before the event. So the earlier you make your contacts the more likely you are to confirm your first choices. Not knowing at an early stage who your speakers will be delays distribution of the advance program.

There are several reasons speakers and panelists may decide an invitation suits their purposes so Speakers Committees have to make sure potential speakers are aware of the advantages involved. Usually acceptance is based on such factors as:

> A new audience or exposure opportunity
> Advancement or promotion opportunities
> Prestige of addressing a renowned organization
> Remuneration — honorarium or expenses, or both

The fun begins when the Speakers Committee starts to negotiate with all speakers and panelists. Of course, early contact — months before the conference begins — is essential. The longer the delay, the less the opportunity of obtaining maximum-impact people. Remember, politicians like to keep their options open. They usually are hard to pin down until one or two months before the conference is scheduled to start. If a political figure cannot give a firm decision, what is really being said is: "If a better opening doesn't come along and there is no trouble on the floor of the House, I might just take you up on your offer."

Telephone calls are best for initial contacts. Neither party is legally or morally committed to anything — unless enthusiasm carries you away in the urge to land a speaker. There are several "musts" to be observed. Provide the following data:

> Date, day, hour, place
> Good description of your organization
> Conference objectives, themes and other speakers
> Specific topic suggestions
> Honorarium, accommodation and travel arrangements
> If the arrangements will or will not include a guest

Keep your side of the conversation brief. Let the speaker have his or her say to determine the interest in your proposal. If a tentative acceptance is given, your immediate goal has been achieved.

The telephone process must be repeated until the Committee has surveyed some 120 per cent of actual speaker, lecturer and panelist needs. Fallout is heaviest a few months prior to the conference.

Once all telephone data is complete, the Committee should make a formal analysis of every potential speaker. Each has to be considered according to prominence, relevance, delivery, international and national reputation, newsworthiness and ability to deliver his or her message.

This also implies a sensitive rating of every preliminary acceptance. By using speaker-rating sheets the process of choosing program slots becomes a little more rational. Obviously, excellent speakers are good bets for getting the conference off and running. Soloists or panelists of similar caliber should start proceedings every morning and afternoon. The top speakers are usually reserved for dinner events.

Be wise. Speakers are unwelcome at breakfasts. Even professional comedians balk at the 8:00 A.M. kickoff breakfast amid sleepy delegates. By the way, have you ever attended a convention with a second or third dinner speaker? If one person cannot say it well, two or three more will not make the picture any clearer.

If it looks like an action-packed morning and afternoon speakers' program, save delegates from instant boredom. Provide dinner speakers and eliminate luncheon talks.

Final speaker lockup is straightforward, provided that honorariums, accommodation and travel expenses are within the budget. Personal visits and hearing speech tapes are other ways of entering final speaker negotiations.

As soon as the final selections are complete, confirm everything with letters of agreement. Most of the detail required is a repeat of preliminary telephone conversations. Mail every speaker, lecturer and panelist this information:

> Exact date, day and hour, plus duration
> Hotel location, event location
> Specific subject, question and answer periods
> Type of assignment — solo or panel
> Objectives and themes of conference
> Description of organization and conference
> Delegate profile
> Honorarium, accommodation and travel arrangements

Ask every speaker, lecturer and panelist to provide the Speakers Committee with the following information:

> Written letter of acceptance
> Speaking aids or presentation equipment required
> Agreement to record and distribute speech
> Biography and photos for media distribution
> Hotel accommodation preferences and dates
> Method of travel, arrival and departure times
> Who will accompany speaker
> Payment arrangements

Communications such as this should get replies by return mail. But telephone follow up is essential. Some speakers insist on early notice yet aren't concerned about early acceptance.

Once an acceptance is received reply immediately. The confirming letter to each speaker should cover the following points:

> Payment arrangements
> List of speakers, lecturers and panelists
> Suggested room layout for conference event
> Name, address and telephone number of Host Committee member
> Briefing and rehearsal times.

Remember, your rating sheets will help replace those unable to accept. Getting every speaker, lecturer and panelist confirmed at a very early date is an important Speakers Committee operation. Detailed planning grinds to a halt in several committees until this job is complete. Promotion or Publicity Committees are most affected. Speaker profiles and topics are their key attendance promotion vehicle.

To the Speakers Committee also falls the preparation of introductions which are short and to the point, particularly if all speakers have been well promoted in conference material. Keep in mind conference objectives and themes. Review all speakers' biographical material and brief, introductory scripts will be relatively easy to write.

Good introductions include the speaker's name, title, company or association affiliation, title of presentation and specific background which is pertinent to the talk. Personal information is rarely relevant, so minimize this material, unless it is recent hard news.

While the committee is attending to its introduction script duties, it should also prepare appropriate thank-you scripts based on what each speaker will say. Remember he or she will recognize what the audience reaction is, so it is unnecessary to explain that to the speaker or to the delegates.

Quite frankly, good introductions never exceed 300 words (90 seconds) and 200 words (60 seconds) are more than ample for the most sincere, thank-you remarks. A well-known personality needs little introduction. A five-minute dissertation is neither necessary nor desirable.

Another special task is the selection of gifts for speakers, lecturers and panelists. Skilled convention planners select two price ranges and then purchase sufficient numbers of the two different gifts. The more expensive item goes to every prominent speaker, the lesser-value gift is given to all other participating speakers and panelists. Both gifts might well be plaques or scrolls incorporating the conference logo or the organization's seal. Other excellent gifts can be symbolic of the conference locale, for example, a reproduction of the official state or provincial emblem. But, be it a model, painting, scroll, local product or whatever, all gifts must prominently display — in the official languages of the conference — a recognition text similar to the following:

*IN APPRECIATION*

*TWENTY-FIFTH ANNUAL*
*NORTH AMERICAN PROMOTIONS ASSOCIATION CONFERENCE*
*LANDMARK*

*July 1980*

Here are two useful tips for the Speakers Committee. First, have sufficient committee members on hand to ensure all the needs of your speakers and panelists are met from arrival to departure. Second, remember last-minute speaker or panelist cancellation panic can be avoided by pre-planning. Make advance arrangements for standby speakers with local universities or other organizations to cover emergency situations.

## SPEAKERS COMMITTEE CHECKLIST

Apart from gifts, every speaker, lecturer and panelist must receive special conference courtesies. The Speakers Committee must arrange many of these details with several other working committees. The sample checklist can serve as a guideline.

Conference host assigned from arrival to departure ☐
Pre-registration, flowers or refreshments in room ☐
Conference, program, kit and event tickets ☐
Speaker's receptions ☐
Rehearsal time and facilities ☐
Immediate payment following presentation ☐
Personal thank-you letters ☐
Prepare speakers' sources list ☐
Select major speakers ☐
Choose supplementary speakers ☐
Arrange preliminary contacts ☐
Finalize speakers' selection ☐
Advise Work Sessions Committee of required equipment ☐
Advise Work Sessions Committee of required rooms ☐
Advise Hosting Committee of required accommodations ☐
Obtain biographies ☐
Obtain speech material ☐
Obtain briefing material ☐
Pass copies to Promotion & Media Committees ☐
Advise Services Committee of place cards, signs,
    notice requirements ☐
Preparation Events schedule ☐
Preparation Moderators' and Chairmans' scripts ☐
Alternate speaker and panelist standbys ☐

# 15

Secrets To
## SESSIONS WITH FLAIR

The first consideration of the Work Sessions Committee is to weave established conference objectives and themes into every session presentation. The ultimate goal is to get the most mileage and impact possible out of every speaker, lecturer and panelist.

Several elemental session boundaries and considerations are involved in planning any meeting. They vary, depending on the purpose of the conference. Sales conventions work best when day one is primarily devoted to relaxation and re-establishing friendships. Then promptly at 8:00 A.M. on day two, open up with all guns and state the message. Keep on stating it with increasing rapidity until the conclusion of the last session.

The program format of a political convention is quite different. They often start with plenary sessions, split into policy sessions and then shift into bull sessions to get a second view. The second day is usually reserved for resolution sessions and state-of-the-party addresses. Day three moves delegates back to plenary sessions and finally to voting sessions.

SUCCESSFUL CONFERENCE & CONVENTION PLANNING

In any event Work Sessions Committees have to be pretty hard-nosed when reviewing the recommendations of the Speakers Committees. If certain speakers appear less than adequate suggest alternates before formal invitations are issued. Delegates rarely sit through three or four days of dull talk. In fact, the speaker — rather than the session — is fundamental to success.

Give some thought to basics. How formal should the conference sessions be? Annual meetings do require a degree of formality. But for the summer conference at a resort hotel clothing will be casual except for the few formal events.

Work in one or two scenery changes. It should be made a crime to lock national and international delegates in one hotel for three days or more. Most want to learn the economic, social and political dimensions of the convention locale and see some local color in the process. Schedule outside events for maximum impact.

The day of one-way communication from speakers to delegates is over. Now two-way communication — free discussion between delegates and speakers — is the rule, rather than the exception. Moreover, organizers of some conferences find one-way communication techniques rarely work unless the dialogue is from the delegates to the speakers.

Names, types and purposes of sessions need not be confusing. Cut through the jargon and think of every session as a one-way or a two-way event. There are more than enough formats for the one-way or two-way lecture, panel and group session. A number of variations and additions to the formats suggested here can also be considered.

## TWO-WAY WORK SESSIONS

INTERVIEW/LECTURE: Recommended to create high delegate interest — sometimes called hot-seat or total-involvement. The interviewer has two roles to play — one is to prod audience into the question/ discussion process. Second, posing his or her own questions.

CONFRONTATION/LECTURE: Usually a crunch situation between a controversial expert and a special interest group. A good vehicle for less than 50 people.

INTERROGATION/PANEL: No opening statements. Panelists ask questions of each other and the audience. A hard way to generate dialogue but better than most panel presentation techniques.

OPPOSED/PANEL: Disagreement on panel at the start of pro- ceedings usually creates good delegate response. A great debate generator if moderator involves the audience as quickly as possible.

REVERSE/PANEL: If everything else fails, this may be the only means to get two-way discussion started. The panel questions the audience to obtain their views.

BUZZ/SESSION: The best discussion technique invented to date. Great for late afternoon or evening situations. Groups are restricted to 10 or 12 people.

CLINIC/SESSION: Small round-table demonstration meetings. Nuts and bolts sessions which generate discussion.

CONCURRENT/SESSION: Usually one half-hour each, run three or four times concurrently with three or four other similar sessions. Delegates move from session to session.

GENERAL/SESSION: Usually a speaker, lecturer or film presentation for all attendees. Discussion is usually permitted but is hampered by size of audience.

PLENARY/SESSION: The name indicates formality often imposed at annual meetings, president's reports and inquiries. Some are structured so no discussion is encouraged, except from voting delegates debating motions.

Q & A/SESSION: Enables audience to fill in gaps following any session. If planned, announce them in the conference program, make sure speakers and panelists have all the facts and recognize each questioner in order. Restrict "statement" questions at the beginning.

WORK/SESSION: Groups are limited to 20 individuals. These are the meetings held to thrash out reports, study findings and complete submissions to plenary sessions. Great discussion creator mechanisms.

## ONE-WAY PROGRAM EVENTS

SPEAKER/LECTURE: Discussion opportunities are few and far between. Strictly an "I'm telling you" vehicle, sometimes blunted by a question period.

VISUAL/LECTURE: A modern disguise of the Speaker/Lecture where audiovisuals do the talking. Usually gets maximum delegate attendance. When content is excellent, it is one of the most exciting presentations available.

SPEAKER/PANEL: Panel should leap in — hardly before speaker concludes — and present problems for the audience. If panel and speaker agree everyone goes home unsatisfied.

STRAIGHT/PANEL: Same technique as Speaker/Panel without a major opening speech. Good — if delegates only want assurance that everything is coming up roses.

SOLVER/PANEL: Difficult to generate audience participation. Panel responds to and resolves pre-submitted questions. Danger is panel may respond with prepared answers.

FORUM/SESSION: Two or more panelists communicate their points of view to the audience. Moderator makes summation before audience can ask questions. Discussion rarely encouraged until the official "word" is clearly understood. Also known as Symposium.

SITUATION/SESSION: Just about every sales and marketing department believes in them. Some marketing men refer to them as Role-Playing Situations. Another name is Skill Presentation. Several sales approaches are reviewed and finally you learn the one guaranteed to sell. Use only when every attendee is employed by the sponsoring organization.

Delegate delight is the conference with good session scheduling. Delegate dissatisfaction follows when certain simple fundamentals are ignored. Here are some of the essentials for sessions with snap:

☐ Insist on keeping to the timetable. Every chairman or moderator must start and stop every session on time, maintaining pace.

☐ Each chairman or moderator greets delegates, introduces speakers and panelists, makes announcements, presentations and thanks participants. This is the only technique which ensures sessions are kept on schedule.

☐ Limit panels to four members, so discussions are clear, to the point, and not repetitive.

☐ Compress panel discussion, expand question periods so delegates can participate.

☐ Planted questions, which do not have to be obvious, always break the ice.

☐ Pre-published position papers generate lively discussions.

☐ Tight summations bring delegates back to objectives. Use at policy sessions only.

☐ Answer every question, even the loaded ones, head-on. That is what communication is all about.

☐ Every head-table participant must have a personal microphone to eliminate confusion.

Before a Speakers Committee can wrap up its plans, it has to ask some questions. How many sessions are actually required? How many delegates will attend each session? What type and number of session rooms are available? How big is the equipment and services budget for conference sessions? Will the delegates have to work too much? Are there too many speakers, lecturers and panelists?

Obviously the Speakers Committee must consider delegates first in working with the Program Group. Delegates have the right to maximum participation and speakers have the right to be heard.

There are two basic reasons for conference sessions which bear repeating. Either delegates are meeting to exchange or pool information, or delegates expect to achieve action on the basis of group discussion. In both situations delegates should participate voluntarily, not be requested to speak.

Asking delegates to speak has almost vanished from the conference scene. The trick is to increase involvement by providing delegates with openings which they can take advantage of in their own way.

Similarly, it is a mistake to sum up every session. A good seminar or discussion will conclude without it being necessary for someone to summarize results, apart from resolution or report sessions.

Points such as these emphasize the need for good session chairmen and moderators. They need practice before they perform. Hold rehearsals and stress that conference sessions must be balanced, lively, relaxed and relevant. Moreover, each conference session must be kept under control and on schedule. Concentrate on the following potential problems:

> Foster discussion by examining differences
> Questioning encourages discussion
> Curb yes and no replies
> Keep in check the complaint specialists
> Minimize wandering from the agenda
> Understand each session objective
> Be complimentary as often as possible
> Avoid personal opinion

If conference chairmen and moderators follow these guidelines, delegates will have maximum opportunity for involvement. Participation is the password which means getting the most out of every work session.

## SESSIONS COMMITTEE CHECKLIST

| | |
|---|---|
| Analyze conference meeting rooms and equipment | ☐ |
| Select each session format | ☐ |
| Coordinate with Speakers Committee to determine speaking, panel and session needs | ☐ |
| Advise Services Committee of requirements | ☐ |
| Program each session | ☐ |
| Prepare moderators' and chairmens' sources list | ☐ |
| Select major moderators and chairmen | ☐ |
| Choose supplementary moderators and chairmen | ☐ |
| Arrange session rehearsal times and locations | ☐ |
| Prepare session scripts with Speakers Committee | ☐ |
| Pre-arrange standby moderators and chairmen | ☐ |

# 16

Hurrah for
## THE ANNUAL AWARDS

I t seems annual awards are always a bone of contention. When you hear a comment such as: "Why did Sarah win the Rose Bowl? Abigail was a much better choice", it means: "I should have won the damn thing!"

Discontent, over several years, usually results in demands to increase the number of awards. Finally, almost every convention delegate has three or four trophies in recognition of several inconsequential activities. Organizations have been known to increase the number of award presentations to the point of sheer boredom.

It's a pity the awards business gets so out of hand. Consider, if you will, television coverage of some major award presentations. They seem little more than exercises in mutual adoration and bad scheduling. Keep things in perspective. If there are more than 10 award presentations scheduled for your annual dinner, you may be falling into the awards trap.

Why have awards at all? Most experts agree such public recognition should be based on the following factors:

Public achievement outside the organization
Best annual achievement within the organization — by category
Exceptional long-term service outside the organization
Exceptional long-term service within the organization

Each award must emphasize organization goals, recognize individual accomplishment, promote competition and honor self-improvement. They must also be capable of generating major publicity. If these criteria do not apply, then the awards program should be revised or scrapped.

Awards Committee responsibilities always seem complex — why this should be so it is difficult to understand. An astute chairman with an iron hand is the first requirement, supported by voting members prepared to withhold awards if there are no suitable nominees. In addition there must be agreement — signed in blood, if necessary — that the president and conference chairman are ineligible for all awards.

Keep awards honest. Nominations should be made by the general membership as well as the Awards Committee. Judging sessions should include at least one non-association member to bring perspective. Votes — by secret ballot — are then cast by the Committee, not the membership. The entire process is anything but a popularity contest.

Only two application forms are required: nomination forms and review sheets. The nomination form, containing conditions of all awards and judging, also serves as a conference promotion piece. Therefore, it goes to every association member several months before the convention begins.

Keep in mind that delegate attendance promotion has increased impact when several work sessions are chaired by an award winner. Delegates want full details of the programs that earned awards. Sessions chaired by award-winners are usually the best attended events at modern conventions. Often they result in good feature articles for local and national media. If the Awards Committee agrees make the winners work at the conference sessions.

Award results should be announced and presentations made during the first day of the conference. This is news that must achieve full media coverage for its own sake. Also, it means immediate presentation of high-impact material to all delegates. Avoid award presentations on annual election day or policy-formation day, if maximum media impact is what you want.

Winners should always be informed in confidence — well before the event — by the Awards Committee. This ensures attendance and avoids potential embarrassment. If award winners fail to show media interest will falter. Apart from that, there has on occasion been the winner who has refused an award — right at the moment of presentation — stating that someone else is more deserving. A comment bound to get wide media coverage!

Biographies and photographs of the winners have to be obtained as soon as acknowledgments are received. This material is so essential to publicity it is a wonder it is so often overlooked. Certainly, the old argument that winners must not know until the very last moment has little logic.

Awards Committees with experience realize news releases are a necessity. The media should not be expected to obtain this material from the winners. Media time is better expended on other conference coverage. It is also one of the reasons most organizations fail to receive maximum awards publicity on a local or national basis.

If Award Workshops are planned the Sessions Committee has to know the names of all winners in advance. The committee requires presentation, equipment needs and room size particulars so it can develop sessions for fullest impact.

Finally, standardize the size, shape, style and cost of all awards. Care and thought is required if awards are to stand the test of time and reflect historic, current and long-range goals of the association. Check the ground rules for speakers' gifts outlined on page 93 of Chapter 14. The basic considerations are remarkably similar.

## AWARDS COMMITTEE CHECKLIST

Review existing awards competition policy ☐
Propose policy amendments if necessary ☐
Redesign awards if necessary ☐
Coordinate award events with Program Group ☐
Prepare awards competition publicity ☐
Prepare awards program entry forms ☐
Schedule awards sessions ☐
Coordinate sessions with Sessions Committee ☐
Obtain Winners' biographies and photographs ☐
Prepare news release material for Media Committee ☐
Advise winners of their session assignments ☐

# 17

## The Science of
# EATING, DRINKING AND BEING MERRY

t happened. The Conference Committee selected a hockey arena during the summer for a breakfast planned for the middle of winter! Embarrassed apologies did little to satisfy delegates, seated on metal chairs, placed on half-inch plywood which had been laid directly over the ice. Believe it or not, the 56°F/13°C room temperature was slightly warmer than the hotcakes.

Obviously, convention confusion crops up at events scheduled purely for entertainment and haphazardly slotted into the program without regard to delegate needs. All meal and entertainment events have to be keyed to conference objectives and themes.

Is it humanly possible to satisfy everyone's tastes in entertainment, meals, receptions and the like? Hardly. Events Committees should accept this as fact and begin researching. Is something that's fun and educational necessary beyond the conference itself? Will events for the entire family mean greater conference attendance? Will breakfasts assure early morning participation? Should luncheons be formal or informal events? But before getting involved in entertainment and event planning there is the matter of budget.

SUCCESSFUL CONFERENCE & CONVENTION PLANNING

Registration fees should entitle delegates to attend all events. Additional costs for special events generate dissatisfaction. It may exclude some people because they can't afford to pay for extras. By the same token, hold concurrent all-delegate luncheons when the executive meets separately at a private lunch so everyone receives the same benefits as the senior representatives.

When faced with a no-sponsors policy or severe budget limitations, reduce entertainment, meals and receptions. Concentrate on one major happening a day so everyone gets a break from the regular proceedings. It's thoughts such as these which emphasize the need for a sponsored-events policy at almost every convention.

Events Committees will discover their personal preferences rarely appeal to everyone. What strikes one person as the perfect meal might well be unpalatable to the multitude. Check with a dietician to ensure balanced and nutritious meals. How about kosher meals or food for diabetics and those with allergies? You will need to arrange special service for these people.

Keep in mind that it is only convention and resort hotels that plan menus for extended-stay guests. Many downtown hotels offer three daily meals, each consisting of five to six courses. As a result, you have over-fed, weary delegates and probably conference over-spending. If sponsored breakfasts are planned, go for a hearty buffet, and plan lunch as a light, inexpensive repast. The money you save will provide a feast in the evening. Remember, light breakfasts and lunches mean delegates will stay awake during the day's sessions.

Isolated breakfast/luncheon/dinner menu planning is dangerous, particularly when all meals are selected directly from the standard list of hotel menu suggestions. Hold one or two food events outside the hotel, prepared by another chef. If an outdoor setting is chosen plan an alternative site. The annual banquet implies the best in food, service and atmosphere. Every other food event is secondary.

Meal costs are very important. Hotels often permit switching or deleting menu items to provide a more reasonable price per plate estimate. If the budget is small, let delegates pay for their own breakfasts before considering low-priced evening meals.

By the same reasoning, low-cost food suffers in quantity and quality. Luncheon buffets are fun but experienced convention planners know there is little saving when compared to regular hotel plate prices.

Arrive at agreed meal costs with the convention hotel for service at a date some six to ten months hence. If the catering manager hesitates request a current price figure. Be prepared for potential 20 per cent cost-per-plate increases. One recent convention committee saw meal prices rise three times in 15 months. If you are determined to budget in a responsible manner seek this information early.

Conference dining room atmospheres are just as important as any other item. Informal breakfasts are great in open, sun-lit rooms. Formal dinners with spot-lit head tables in draped halls are most impressive, but only when external light is held to a minimum.

And there are all manner of rationales for reserved tables, few of which are very credible. Good conference planning suggests everyone, other than head-table guests, is equal. There is one exception only — tables close to the exit should be reserved for conference staff who have to be in seven places at once.

Except for the head table, round tables are recommended. Be sure each dining room will accommodate all delegates comfortably. Mess hall set-ups will destroy the best dining environment the Events Committee can achieve.

The timing of dining events is a science in itself. Food service, speeches and entertainment must be scheduled to the minute. Remarks from the head table are taboo when food is being served or eaten. Head-table guests should eat with everyone else, rather than before or after. Meals move quickly when the first course is pre-set. Check the timing with the hotel catering manager to minimize conflict and confusion. The Events Committee must work very closely with other Program Group Committees on these details.

Quite apart from menu selection, room sizes and layouts, the Events Committee is also concerned with a number of regulations and restrictions. Essential information includes entertainment and liquor legislation, hotel regulations, performers' union requirements and a host of other seemingly strange rules, but everyday facts of life at the convention site.

State and provincial liquor laws have been broadened significantly in recent years. In some cities beverages are available 24 hours a day, seven days a week, except on election days. Ten chances to one that's not the case at your conference site. So tailor events involving refreshments accordingly and know the regulations as if you are expecting to appear in court.

Cocktail parties, beer and wine receptions do work, if they are well controlled. Half an hour — no more than 45 minutes at most — is long enough before luncheons and dinners. Rent a room large enough to accommodate everyone. The bar set up and staffing arrangements should be on a two-drink per person basis. Have sufficient mix on hand, as there will be people who prefer soft drinks or juices to alcohol. Holding receptions in the exhibit hall is a great help to the Exhibits Committee.

Late evening events should be closed down after an hour and a half. Don't hesitate over the exact moment of closing. Have the hotel unobtrusively withdraw the bars, one at a time, starting fifteen minutes before the reception finale. One or two drinks more could mean trouble.

Observe protocol if state or provincial dignitaries have been invited.

In some areas, bars must stay open as long as the governor or lieutenant governor is in the room. These functions can, and have, continued until 3:00 A.M.!

Check hotel reception regulations very carefully. Some will not permit donated or complimentary liquor on their premises, and most hotels have varying prices for one ounce as compared to one-and-one quarter ounce drinks. Other hotels charge for every open bottle remaining in the bar; and they keep the open bottles for the next reception at additional cost.

The best way through this maze is to come to total-price agreements for every reception. Advise the hotel of the number of anticipated delegates and then state you want a firm price for appetizers, two drinks, room rental, bartenders, waitresses, tax and tips. When the money runs out the reception is over. And demand a rebate clause for receptions which are closed down early.

If wine is to be served at a dinner consider omitting the pre-meal reception unless the reception features the wines for the meal. If money is really no object some conferences schedule stunning, champagne breakfasts.

A word regarding hospitality suites. They are prone to get out of hand unless supervised with tact and decorum. Appoint one Events Committee member to monitor opening and closing hours. Conflicts arise when VIP delegates are celebrating and the other delegates are trying to sleep in adjoining rooms. And always ensure you are dealing with reputable sponsors.

Drop-in-suites — where coffee and sandwiches are available, along with magazines and promotional material — are conference winners. Seek one sponsor for delegates, one for spouses and one for children. Exhibits, color television, soft drinks, entertainment and games are good youth-involvement builders. Stand-up breakfast suites at 7:00 A.M. and 10:00 P.M. coffee and sandwich suites are used with great success today by low-key sponsors.

Conference entertainment is a necessity. All sessions and no relaxation make Jack and Jill Delegates dull. Good value comes from hiring entertainers who specialize in material appropriate to the age of the audience. Comedy fashion shows — provided they are well-scripted and clothing can be purchased at reasonable cost — make for added interest. It is wise to have an outside specialist run fashion shows as the Events Committee probably has more than enough work as it is.

Costume get-togethers are great. Included in this category are Las Vegas Nights, Roaring Twenties' Balls, Saloon Evenings and Harem Parties. Better still is to tie the costume affair into the conference theme. The pre-conference program should detail this event, advising where costumes can be rented. For maximum efficiency, set up a separate room in the hotel and have a costume rental company bring their garments and staff to the premises. Black tie and tuxedo rentals can be handled in the same manner.

And a few reminders. Comedy acts in good taste are hard to beat. But what you think is acceptable entertainment may well be considered exotic or erotic by others. Safest are comedy skits with little emphasis on innuendo or double meanings. Accept the fact that you must make standby entertainment arrangements in case of no-shows. Scenery is important in setting the mood. Of course, you must check union regulations and requirements before hiring any performers.

Even the best entertainment events can backfire if certain guidelines are ignored. Avoid second-rate performers. Consider all entertainment possibilities to determine what would suit the occasion. Visit every facility before booking theatres, night clubs, museums, planetariums or art galleries. Hiring talent agencies sight unseen is a risky undertaking. Employing association or committee members who consider themselves comedians is even worse. Book name acts strictly on reputation.

Meanwhile, back at the conference hotel, appreciate that catering managers require early attendance estimates for each event, so food, drink and supplies can be purchased and arrangements made for adequate staff. The earlier these estimates are completed by the Committee, the better. Anticipate that attendance can vary at each function. Delegates will be inviting guests to important sessions and major dinner events. They may bypass certain sessions — particularly if they want to see local attractions.

One month before the conference attendance estimates must be pretty firm. But 24 hours or more before each function an exact estimate must be given to the hotel. This number, multiplied by the agreed cost per plate, is the invoice amount — plus tax and tip. Even if some delegates fail to show you will be charged for the meals you guaranteed.

If there is a small overflow, the hotel can usually accommodate extra servings with little disturbance. However, large overruns cause trouble. Additional tables have to be set up, servers are overworked and chefs have to prepare extra servings, often different from the menu.

The Events Committee must be conservative and honest when it gives hotel management final attendance estimates. Raise or lower estimates for each event based on actual counts from events held 24 hours before. You owe this courtesy to the sponsor, the hotel, the delegates, the speaker and your association.

Be precise. Head counts are the only way Events Committees know they are receiving accurate billing. Cooperate with the Finance Committee in this area. Count heads when the hotel counts heads—at the door or during the event—and come to an immediate agreement. Event tickets help minimize this elementary problem.

Meal and refreshments events are the barometer of every conference committee's ability to act as a good and generous host. Devote as much research and planning time to these events as is spent on the educational segments of the program. With proper planning these functions help set the pace, reinforce goals and enhance the tone of the sessions. In fact, meal and refreshment events can kindle delegate interest anew throughout the program.

Coffee breaks are important. Schedule one every morning to maintain high attention levels, and one in the afternoon if time permits. Keep coffee setups in areas adjacent to meeting rooms so delegates are not disturbed. Allow 15 minutes only for these breaks. Do this by increasing the number of urns and/or servers, according to the audience size.

And work on the premise that sufficient time must be allotted at the opening of the conference for get-acquainted purposes. It is important for delegates to catch up on news and on old friends before turning to the business at hand.

Fortunately, many North American hotels today take pride in serving a wide variety of international menus. Thus, Events Committees have a multitude of dining options. The following meal suggestions are only a sample of what you can accomplish. Variety and balance are essential.

## SAMPLE MENU SUGGESTIONS

WEDNESDAY
*8:00 a.m. - 9:30 a.m.*
Eye-Opener Breakfast - Buffet, Hotel Ballroom #7
    MENU: Apple, Orange, Tomato Juice
                Scrambled Eggs, Bacon
                White or Whole Wheat Toast, Jam
                Coffee, Tea, Milk
*12:30 p.m. - 1:45 p.m.*
Lift-Off Lunch - Hotel Ballroom #5
    MENU: Tomato Juice
                Baked Chicken Pot Pie with Carrots, Peas, Potatoes and
                  Mushrooms
                Cole Slaw
                Rolls and Butter
                Strawberry Coupe
                Coffee, Tea, Milk
*6:00 p.m. - 8:30 p.m.*
National Past Presidents' Dinner - Hotel Ballroom #1
    MENU: Celery and Olives
                Stuffed Egg Niçoise
                Consommé En Tasse
                Filet Mignon, Maître D'Hotel
                Persilé Potatoes
                French Green Beans

Rolls and Butter
Cherry Cheese Cake
Coffee, Tea, Milk

THURSDAY
*7:30 a.m. - 9:00 a.m.*
Bright-Eye Buffet, Hotel Ballroom #3
MENU: Grapefruit, Prune, Tomato Juice
Cold Cereals
Sausages and Eggs
Corn, Bran or Blueberry Muffins, Jam, Marmalade
Coffee, Tea, Milk

*9:00 a.m. - 2:00 p.m.*
Box Lunch - Lemoine Park Zoo/Out-Of-Hotel Event
MENU: Cold Meat Plate
Potato Salad
Maçédoine Salad
Pickled Beets
Rolls and Butter
Petit Fours
Coffee, Tea, Milk

*7:00 p.m. - 9:00 p.m.*
National Awards Dinner - Hotel Ballroom #2
MENU: Wine served with meal
Celery and Olives
Yellow Pea Soup, Quebecoise
Baked Ham*, with Glazed Pineapple
Au Gratin Potatoes
Broccoli Au Beurre
Tossed Green Salad
Rolls and Butter
Cheese Board with Crackers
Coffee, Tea, Milk

*Ham must be old/fashioned, sugar/cured, not rolled ham.

Variety is the spice that delights delegate palates. Listen carefully to the menu specialists at your conference site.

---

## EVENTS COMMITTEE CHECKLIST

| | |
|---|---|
| Screen delegate food preferences | ☐ |
| Check for special diets | ☐ |
| Select formal and informal events | ☐ |
| Determine event costs for approval by Budget Committee | ☐ |
| Check regulations, policies, customs and permits necessary for each event: | ☐ |

| | | | |
|---|---|---|---|
| Federal | ☐ | Union | ☐ |
| State | ☐ | Hotel | ☐ |

Provincial ☐     Organization ☐
Municipal ☐
Plan receptions ☐
Determine menus ☐
Determine coffee breaks ☐
Prepare contracts for meals, receptions and entertainment ☐
Advise Services Committee of needs ☐
Advise hotel of final attendance 24 hours before each event ☐
Confirm attendance counts with hotel at each event ☐
Verify attendance counts with Budget Committee ☐

Not To Forget
# SPOUSES AND FAMILIES

**R**ecent hotel statistics confirm delegates continue to combine family vacations with annual conferences. Summer sessions at resort hotels mean high family attendance, but even in mid-winter, when the weather is suitable, family involvement is apparent. Moreover, promoting spouse and family programs can increase conference attendance to say nothing of larger audiences at individual events.

Organizations experienced in family conference planning know that spouses are very interested participants. Spouses are welcome at all sessions and provided with session tickets. Breakfasts are usually family affairs. So, take a tip from these experts. Throw in one or two full-family dinners and trust the parents to be the best judge of their children's bahavior.

Always think of Spouses Committees — *never* Ladies or Guest Committees. Quite often today the delegate is a woman who has invited her spouse as a guest. This alone proves the value of undertaking research. The Spouses Committee has to investigate potential family attendees and determine their preferences. Of course, it also implies checking main events to see how they can be adjusted to accommodate everyone.

Good Spouses Committees coordinate their plans with the Finance and Sponsors Committees. Remember, events for spouses require funds to ensure success. Registration fees are a necessity, but when these are set too high delegates may leave their families at home.

Even at a delegates-only conference it is wise to set up a spouses' lounge and a children's room with entertainment and staff. Far better to cancel these facilities for non-attendance rather than scrambling to set up facilities the morning the convention gets under way.

If children's ages vary widely, two rooms will be necessary. For the younger set, plan one area with interesting games and organized activities. Set up the room for the older group to include such diversions as guitar instruction, records, television and soft drinks. These lounges work best when staffed by children of local committee members. Supervision must be minimal. An adult committee worker in the background is more than enough for control.

For some, lectures are valuable, particularly when related to current problems affecting the family. There is high interest today in sessions dealing with drugs, sensitivity training, economics, pornography, ecology, environment health or education. Look for in-the-know speakers to create group discussion opportunities. Include special sessions where spouses can better understand business or labor.

Sherry, port or wine parties featuring new brands, hosted by sponsors, should be considered. Top results are guaranteed when sponsors explain and demonstrate their products.

Swimming pool events are another possibility. Apart from reserving the pool, little organization is required if it is an in-hotel event. Families can entertain themselves but make arrangements with the local swim or diving team to stage a short display. If a committee member owns a private pool which can accommodate the group so much the better. This means another out-of-hotel event. Play it safe, heated pools are best. But even then you can't be sure. Delegates at one recent convention learned it takes at least 24 hours to heat a swimming pool to an acceptable temperature.

Television is always a popular entertainment but heighten interest by arranging a tour of the local television facility or a live audience viewing.

House and garden tours generate considerable interest particularly when the famous and historic mansions are included. Indoor tours are tricky in northern areas during winter. What with boots, coats, and hats you have to plan these events very carefully.

Sight-seeing events are standard at most conferences. They are best programmed as tours to and from out-of-hotel sessions and events. Charter buses with professional tour conductors, PA systems and, if possible, on-bus washrooms. Lots of walk and go stops, plus appropriate literature increase interest. Caution—most bus outings are too long. One and one-half hours is adequate to see the highlights of most cities. Visiting historic sites can take a little longer provided a lunch is included.

Shopping tours and fashion shows are very common. But remember that most people prefer to shop on their own. Provide lists of stores and their merchandise and set up free time for these activities. Schedule transportation for everyone if shopping is far removed from the convention hotel.

Tea or coffee parties can be dull unless they are tied into a special occasion such as meeting a celebrity. An event to meet other delegates' spouses isn't enough, particularly when a get-acquainted reception was scheduled the night before.

Bingo, bridge, auction 45 and other games rarely generate guest enthusiasm. If they must be a part of the program consider hiring a tournament expert to provide instruction and manage the event.

Many nightclubs, operas and theatres offer group discounts. Why not include these in your free evening suggestions for delegates?

Shopping center tours for teens are appealing, especially if they get behind the scenes to visit stock rooms, delivery rooms and kitchens, as well as learning how security staff handle various shopping center situations. Find something different. Avoid the events which they get in the classroom.

Out-of-conference transportation is a significant expense item. Chartered buses continue to be the most cost-effective means of transport. Head counts are easier and less convention staff is required. Bus expenses can often be sponsored. Talk to local transit officials, convention bureaus or potential sponsors who might underwrite a transportation deal.

It is customary to give prizes and gifts to spouses and children. If several items are involved present them in a single package. Many convention bureaus have extensive lists of free or low-cost conference stuffer material. Select gifts for your delegates which meet your conference criteria.

Avoid the pitfalls of crack-of-dawn events. Continuous, day-long programs leave everyone overly organized. Rush hour bus tours delay other conference events. Don't run any spouses' events to 5:00 P.M. Attendees will have no time to get ready for evening functions.

Organize hospitality lounges. Create separate parent and children's committees. Hold a night bus tour for children and teenagers. Organize an out-of-hotel teen event the moment delegates arrive so mother or father can get some rest.

Prepare special promotion mailers for the Printing Committee. Mail them to the family address. Send follow-up letters. Have name tags available when spouses and children register. Distribute spouses' and children's rosters which list names, home towns and room numbers.

Organize family events with a fine-edge sophistication. Plan high-interest activity during the first days of the conference when the family is fresh and enthusiastic. But, remember some people prefer to relax and be on their own. Spouses Committees have to plan alternatives as most families want to do a little of both.

### SPOUSES COMMITTEE CHECKLIST

Research spouses and children ☐
Cost estimate all functions ☐
Hire local experts ☐
Hospitality suites ☐
Prepare publicity ☐
Conference program information ☐
Prepare invitations ☐
Conference kits for spouses and children ☐
Spouses invitation for all conference sessions ☐
Select gifts and prizes ☐
Coordinate all events with Program Group ☐

# 19

Results with
## PROMOTION
## AND PUBLICITY

ne goal, one objective, one purpose—promote delegate attendance. That's the single responsibility of every Promotion Committee. Study the audience involved and generate a meaningful publicity program which will ensure maximum convention attendance.

The target audience—the people who might attend the conference—is composed of several publics. Delegates, employers, sponsors, government, private enterprise, the media and a host of other special interest groups are involved in every convention. Specific promotion programs are required for each of these groups to ensure they will attend and participate.

Take a hard look at your target audience. Why did last year's conference have a high or low attendance? How many employers sponsored convention delegates? Why were there so many exhibitors on hand? What will interest private enterprise? How can the Promotion Committee be sure of a good family turnout?

Obviously promotion means different things to different segments of the audience. Plan separate promotion programs and conference attendance will increase accordingly.

Promotion means advance information. And, publicity programs have to be informative, as well as varied. Emphasize the positive. Stress improvement and change. Split mail all material. Send conference objectives and speakers' names to business addresses. Family informaticn is strictly for home consumption. One major American management conference promotes only a five-point agenda, 25 speakers and 10 work sessions. Fun and games aren't mentioned at all. These conference sponsors know management is not impressed with fun and frippery. Stress training and education benefits to management if you expect delegate costs to be underwritten.

Tourist promotion kits make handsome packages and are easy to acquire for all prospective delegates. But they seldom promote conferences effectively. Stress the program and the speakers. If vital statistics and information are packed into promotion material, the Promotion Committee will sell the conference. Plan promotion moments for the next convention as the current sessions are coming to an end. Delegates attending this year's conference are the most likely prospects for next year. Obtain a conference roster and contact this group early.

A few words of caution. Minimize extensive, long-range promotion. Otherwise you have nothing new or important to convey during the many months before your convention gets under way.

Coming on with all public relations stops pulled out during prior conventions will lose you delegates and friends. You might even undermine or diminish objectives and themes of the conference that is currently in session.

Promotion in good taste works. Consider conference reminders tied to commemorative postage stamp issues, discounts for early registration, prizes to local member societies with highest per capita registration and letters saying "I'm going because,"..followed with a list of attendance reasons penned by VIPs.

Visit local societies and chapters during their regular monthly meetings, sponsor sandwich and coffee receptions for target audiences across the country. Appoint local society promotion chairmen and provide them with promotion material. Personal contact far outweighs the impact of promotion-by-mail programs.

Crack the barrier. Make every effort to register those who were not at last year's sessions. Tell them your conference is breaking new ground.

Publicity continues on the convention floor. Public relations consultants are a necessity here. They can publish one or two tabloid editions for delivery to every delegate's room before breakfast. The PR consultants will know how to keep it simple. Much of the work can be done well in advance by gathering photos of the executive members from across the country. This material can be augmented with prewritten background stories on the association and interesting members. The delegates roster can also be included. The history of the organization can also be prepared in advance. The bulletin is completed with a record of daily convention happenings.

Delegates are pleased to see bulletins tucked under their doors. It means public relations people working in the wee hours but it has always proved a worthwhile technique.

If you plan to shoot the publicity works, contact advertising departments of the major newspapers in the community and develop a convention supplement. One recent supplement contained 12 pages, crammed with 18 photographs, 25 stories and 53 advertisements. Three of the ads were full-page. Some 80,000 households received the supplement, encouraging attendance at exhibits and opening sessions. The association received 10 per cent of all advertisement revenues.

Note that there is little alternative to the step-by-step chain of events which all Promotion Committees must follow.

## PROMOTION COMMITTEE SCHEDULES

FIRST ANNOUNCEMENT: Tell who, what, where, when and why — use mailers, news releases.

SECOND ANNOUNCEMENT: Release draft program and hotel information. Tightly-edited business mailers.

THIRD ANNOUNCEMENT: Release family mailer to home addresses.

FIRST PERSONAL CONTACT: Chairman visits all member organizations. Visual presentations, receptions, tourist packages.

FOURTH ANNOUNCEMENT: Release awards competition material. Use mailers, news releases, trade journal articles and advertising.

FIFTH ANNOUNCEMENT: Release information on speakers and work sessions, conference registration and hotel accommodation forms. Mailers, news releases — business addresses only.

SPOUSES ANNOUNCEMENT: Release detailed information on programs at same time as FIFTH ANNOUNCEMENT. Home addresses only.

SIXTH ANNOUNCEMENT: Reminder of awards cut-off-date and registration deadline. Announce number of delegates registered to date.

SEVENTH ANNOUNCEMENT: Personal invitation from civic, state or provincial officials. Mailers to home addresses.

EIGHTH ANNOUNCEMENT: Reminder of registration date. Mailers to business addresses.

NINTH ANNOUNCEMENT: Registration cut-off date reminder. Gimmick mailer. Mailers to both business and home addresses.

TENTH ANNOUNCEMENT: Final registration deadline. Number of delegates registered to date. Home address list.

## PROMOTION COMMITTEE CHECKLIST

Identify promotion programs which will create
convention interest and involvement ☐
Concentrate on last year's delegates ☐
Devise promotion ideas for absentees ☐
Prepare promotion schedule ☐
Develop promotion kits ☐
Schedule promotion events across country ☐
Obtain tourist literature ☐
Obtain hotel literature ☐
Obtain conference literature ☐
Schedule mailings with Program Committee ☐

# 20

The Convention –
## PUTTING IT IN PRINT

**L**ittle things mean a lot. Conference print materials should be uniform in design, color, style and type. Convention materials are instantly recognizable when the Print Committee uses techniques which reinforce the many messages to sponsors, delegates, speakers, committee workers and the media.

First, the Committee should list every print message it requires for conference purposes. From this comes a better appreciation of the up-to-date print techniques required during the coming months. Consider the following items:

Advertising
Awards
Badges
Banners
Briefcases
Contracts
Decals
Envelopes

Event Tickets
Flags
Forms
Letterheads
Logos
Menus
Notebooks
Notice Boards
Place Cards
Programs
Ribbons
Signs

Detail all your print requirements, giving full specifications, in one tender package and ask for bids from reputable companies. Using a single printer means style uniformity for every printed item. Standardized logo, typeface, color and design convey a professional impression of your convention.

Delegate badges are a good example. Remember, delegates deserve professional-looking badges—colorful and readable. There are several alternatives: plastic, metal, clear plastic with inserts, ribbons, adhesive cloth and pocket cards. There are drawbacks to each type of identification. Women have handbags, not pockets. Pin badges may tear clothing. Adhesive badges seldom last more than a day and some glues can damage clothing or handbags. Many of these problems can be resolved by purchasing swivel clip/neck chain badges. Have badge companies submit samples of several types and select the one within your budget which will minimize delegate complaints.

Before making final decisions remember there must be plenty of space on tags and badges for personal identification. Names should be typed, not written—for this use special conference typewriters. In North America first names are a must. Extra space may be required for company and home town identification.

Cut costs by soliciting briefcase, notebook, pen and pencil sponsors. Organizations supply these for publicity purposes and may well be pleased to allow your committee to print additional conference particulars. Some sponsors will even incorporate your text on items such as briefcases—at no cost to the conference.

The final delegates' program must be a work of art. Like conference badges, it is one of the most prominent print items on the convention floor. Select a good quality paper stock and be sure to provide the following particulars:

Convention name, logo, place and dates
Function room plans
Conference welcome message

Name, time, location of all sessions and events
Names and titles of organization or association officers
Names of all sponsors, exhibitors and suppliers
Convention dress details
Admission ticket details
Information center details
Spouses' and Children's program details
Names and titles of all conference committee chairmen

Layout and design of the delegates' program are important. Seek professional advice on these particulars. Size is crucial. Programs are carried by delegates throughout the conference. Those four inches by eight inches or less will conveniently fit pockets and handbags.

Pay attention to the national or international nature and location of the convention. There may be need for print materials in one or more languages, depending on home countries of the delegates. In Canada it is customary to print everything in the country's two official languages, French and English.

Because of these language considerations the Print Committee is the best group to assume responsibility for translation services. Spare no expense here—accurate translation is an absolute must.

Avoid all self-appointed translators and interpreters including professors, teachers and your committee or association members. Some print houses have translators but even these professionals can cause problems. For total assurance that foreign language copy is correct, send advance copies of all translated material to senior foreign delegates for final approval before going to print. Simultaneous translation plays an important role at many conventions. When interpreters are required look for professionals listed in the yellow pages of local telephone directories. Check their set-up requirements. You may have to book meeting rooms a day in advance.

Many programs have a sufficient number of pages to print a full day's schedule on a single page. It minimizes confusion—particularly when each page is given a different color. Consider the following representative sample:

25th NATIONAL
CONVENTION
L A N D M A R K
JULY 9, 10, 11, 12, 19—
P R O M O T I O N   I N   T H E   80s
THE NORTH AMERICAN PROMOTIONS ASSOCIATION


WELCOME TO PROMOTION IN THE 80s

The Landmark Committee is pleased to welcome you to PROMOTION IN THE 80s. This year our program events reflect the greater opportunities and challenges facing our profession. During our business sessions, we will examine information and trends in contemporary society.

It is our hope that each of you will take home from this convention new ideas, improved understanding and fond memories of Landmark.

Your Convention Committee

FUNCTION ROOMS AND THEIR
LOCATIONS, BENSON BAY HOTEL

| | |
|---|---|
| Main Floor: | Logan Room |
| | Table and Tankard |
| | Cafeteria Benson |
| | Dutch Boy Lounge |
| Mezzanine Floor: | La Blanche Room |
| | Atlanta Room |
| | Washington Room |
| 1st Floor: | Salons — A, B, C, D |
| 2nd Floor: | Crystal Ballroom |
| | Exhibit Lounge |
| | News Headquarters |
| | Registration and Information |
| | Hunt Room |
| | Hound Room |

WEDNESDAY, JULY 9

| | | |
|---|---|---|
| 8:00 a.m. - 9:30 a.m. | - | Eye-Opener Breakfast (Crystal Ballroom, 2nd Floor) Informal buffet for delegates and families. |
| 9:00 a.m. - 10:00 p.m. | - | Registration, 2nd Floor |
| 9:00 a.m. - 10:00 p.m. | - | Information Center, 2nd Floor General information, appointments, baby sitters, etc. |
| 10:00 a.m. - 11:00 a.m. | - | I Love Music (Hunt Room, 2nd Floor) For swingers of all ages. |
| 10:00 a.m. - 12:00 noon | - | National Council Meeting (Hound Room, 2nd Floor) Directors only. |
| 12:00 noon- 12:30 p.m. | - | Presenting the Presidents (Exhibit Lounge, 2nd Floor) Welcome reception for delegates and spouses. |
| 12:30 p.m. - 1:45 p.m. | - | Lift-Off Luncheon (Crystal Ballroom, 2nd Floor) Informal lunch and entertainment for delegates and families. Chairman — Don Jones, Macon, Georgia Greetings — Mayor Steve Jensen, City of Landmark |
| 2:00 p.m. - 10:00 p.m. | - | Young-As-You-Are Party (Bus at hotel front entrance) For the young set and their friends. |
| 2:30 p.m. - 4:00 p.m. | - | Ladies Get-Acquainted (Suite 610, 6th Floor) Artists' and Authors' Party. |
| 2:30 p.m. - 5:00 p.m. | - | Specialists Sessions. Delegates can attend sessions of their choice. CONSULTANTS: Judy Kent, Toronto, Ontario (Hunt Room, 2nd Floor) GOVERNMENTS: George Rees, Denver, Colorado (Ballroom, 2nd Floor) ORGANIZATIONS: Jean Lafavre, Montreal, Quebec (La Blanche Room, Mezzanine Floor) CORPORATIONS: Keith Bradley, San Francisco, California (Exhibit Lounge, 2nd Floor) |
| 6:30 p.m. - 8:30 p.m. | - | National Past Presidents' Dinner (Crystal Ballroom 2nd Floor) CHAIRMAN: Neville Wilson, Winnipeg, Manitoba SPEAKER: Blake I. Olson, President, Institute of Foreign Affairs, New York, New York |
| 9:00 p.m. - 10:30 p.m. | - | National Past Presidents' Reception and tour of exhibits for delegates and spouses. (Exhibit Lounge, 2nd Floor) |

THURSDAY, JULY 10

| | | |
|---|---|---|
| 7:30 a.m. - 9:00 a.m. | - | Bright-Eye Buffet (Logan Room, Main Floor) For delegates and families. |
| 9:00 a.m. - 12:00 noon | - | Annual Meeting (Crystal Ballroom, 2nd Floor) |
| 9:00 a.m. - 2:00 p.m. | - | Zoo-Do, Lemoine Park (Bus, hotel front entrance) Fun, games and lunch. Dress casual. |
| 12:30 p.m. - 2:15 p.m. | - | National Awards of Excellence Luncheon (La Blanche Room, Mezzanine Floor) CHAIRMAN: Margaret Smith, Landmark. AWARDS PRESENTATION: Don Bell, Binghampton, New York. SPEAKER: Guy Gibbard, President, Promotions Association of France, Paris, France. |

PROMOTIONS SESSIONS

| | | |
|---|---|---|
| 2:30 p.m. - 3:30 p.m. | - | Management in the 80s (Crystal Ballroom, 2nd Floor) Ronald Grant, Executive Director, California Institute of Management, Los Angeles, California. Eric Stephens, Vice-President, Cybernetic Services, Brainerd University. Martha Franks, Communications Consultants, Landmark. |
| 2:30 p.m. - 3:30 p.m. | - | The Association and You (Exhibit Lounge, 2nd Floor) Don Hamilton, President, North American Promotions Association of Canada, Montreal, Quebec. Monty Berrigan, President, North American Promotions Association of United States, Woodstock, Maine. |
| 3:45 p.m. - 4:45 p.m. | - | Environment and People (Hunt Room, 2nd Floor) Tom Sherman, Member of Parliament, Ottawa, Can. Lynn Dogood, Publisher, National Publishers Ltd., Chicago, Illinois. Andrea Arnett, Environmental Consultant, Landmark. |
| 3:45 p.m. - 4:45 p.m. | - | Education for Tomorrow (Hound Room, 2nd Floor) Prof. Bill Scott, Smith University, Wyoming. Ruth Johnson, Franklin Associates, Moncton, New Brunswick. |
| 5:30 p.m. - 6:30 p.m. | - | PROMOTION IN THE 80s RECEPTION. (Crystal Ballroom, 2nd Floor) |
| 7:00 p.m. - 9:00 p.m. | - | National Awards Dinner (Logan Room, Main Floor) Delegates and Families. Awards presentation. CHAIRMAN: Lee MacNeil, President, MacNeil & Company, Landmark. SPEAKER: Dawn Rice, Director Personal Relations, Warner Corporation, Chicago, Illinois. |
| 8:30 p.m. - 9:30 p.m. | - | Austrian Film Fun (Exhibit Lounge, 2nd Floor) For the young set. |

FRIDAY, JULY 11

| | |
|---|---|
| 7:00 a.m. - 11:30 a.m. - | Breakfast Cruise. Buses leave hotel front entrance in two groups. Breakfast served on board the Landmark Star. Dress casual. |
| 9:00 a.m. - 11:00 a.m. - | National Council Meeting (Lower deck, Landmark Star). Directors only. |
| 9:00 a.m. - 10:00 a.m. - | History of the Golden West (Upper deck, Landmark Star). Jack Rafters, University of Landmark. |
| 11:00 a.m. - 11:45 a.m. - | Fort Heritage Tour<br>Parading the Colours, Changing the Guard. |
| 11:45 a.m. - 2:00 p.m. - | Agriculture in the 80s<br>Delegates' picnic. Board buses 2:00 p.m. |
| 3:00 p.m. - 5:00 p.m. - | Awards of Excellence Sessions (Salons A, B, C, D, 1st Floor). Delegates in four groups move through half-hour sessions chaired by this year's award winners. |
| 6:00 p.m. - 7:00 p.m. - | President's Reception (Logan Room, Main Floor)<br>For delegates and spouses, Dress optional. |
| 7:00 p.m. - 9:15 p.m. - | Annual Banquet (La Blanche Room, Mezzanine Floor). For delegates and families.<br>CHAIRMAN: Ted Crane, President, Crane Associates, Landmark.<br>SPEAKER: Senator Frank Rasminsky, Washington, D.C. |
| 9:30 p.m. - 10:30 p.m. - | Promotions/Denver Night (Crystal Ballroom, 2nd Floor). Hosted by next year's Convention Committee of Denver, Colorado. |

SATURDAY, JULY 12

9:00 a.m. - 11:00 a.m.  -  Wishing-Well Farewell (Washington Room, Mezzanine Floor). Delegates and spouses attend breakfast buffet.

9:00 a.m. - 11:00 a.m.  -  Youth's Breakfast (Hunt Room, 2nd Floor).

## NATIONAL EXECUTIVE OFFICERS

| President: | 1st Vice-President: | 2nd Vice-President: |
|---|---|---|
| Warren L. Keynes | Ralph J. Harris | Helen D. Wood |
| Calgary Association | Miami Association | Newark Association |
| Immediate Past President: | Secretary: | Treasurer: |
| Susan L. Robertson | Paul R. Smith | Saul D. Goddard |
| Los Alamos Association | Vancouver Association | Chicago Association |

Executive Secretary:
Hans J. de Bohr
Washington Association

## SPONSORS, EXHIBITORS, SUPPLIERS

The following organizations have, through their generous participation, made PROMOTION IN THE 80s possible. Their active interest and support is gratefully acknowledged by the Conference Committee.

| | | |
|---|---|---|
| Air America | CJKY Television | Lafarge Brewery |
| Alaska Paper Company | Dunphy Displays | Ronald-American Limited |
| Austrian Wine Board | Federal State Insurance | Royal Brokerage Company |
| Bank of Missouri | General Supplies | Metropolitan Landmark |
| Benjamin Jewelers | Great American Express | Radio Station CKRO |
| Black Printers | Hudson's Bay Minerals | Radio Station KLKL |
| British Industries Limited | Imperial Machinery | Simpson-Smith Machinery |
| Canadian Pacific | Limited | Western Print Limited |
| Merchants | James Thompson & Sons | Youth Canada Music |

## CONVENTION DRESS

Informal — slacks, sport shirts, T-shirts, jeans, sunsuits are the order of the day. Dress is your preference for receptions and dinners.

For the Promotions/Denver Night, you may want to wear your finest.

## ADMISSION TICKETS

Admission to all functions is by ticket only to eliminate any possible confusion between delegates and other hotel guests. All tickets turned in at each event will be placed in a drum for special draws at The Promotion/Denver Night. These tickets are also necessary for hotel head count purposes.

ALL EVENTS WILL START ON TIME.

## INFORMATION CENTER
The Registration Office and Information Center is located in the Lounge area on the 2nd floor. Direct line telephone numbers are 842-4294 and 842-4295. Conference staff can assist you with appointments, baby sitting, information regarding the Planetarium, the Concert Hall, the Auditorium, the Playhouse, recreation activities, vacationing, places to shop, and how to get there.

## DAY TICKETS
Your associates and friends are invited to attend all functions. Separate tickets for meals, receptions and business sessions can be purchased at the Registration Desk on the 2nd floor.

## CHILDREN
All children's functions will be supervised. Babysitting arrangements can be made through the Registration Desk at delegates' own expense.

## CONVENTION COMMITTEE
Chairman: Ted Crane
Co-Chairman: Lee MacNeil
Committee Chairmen:
Jacques Lemay — Finance
Frank Neville — Work Sessions & Speakers
Ruth Drake — News & Promotion
Rosa Cherniak — Family Group Program
Ida Jones — Registration, Information, Hosting
Ken Saito — Program Announcements
Jack Rowsell — Accommodations
Shirley Hale — Sponsorships
Irving Gold — Events & Entertainment
René Nault — Translation & Printing
Greta Mueller — Displays & Exhibits
John Kuzyk — Services, Equipment & Transportation
Greg Burton — National Awards

Smaller conferences often combine the Print Committee responsibilities with those of the Promotion Committee (Chapter 19) and the Media Committee (Chapter 25). There is merit in this as both Print and Promotion duties are concluded well in advance of the convention. This means there are people available to undertake other responsibilities. The three workloads are quite similar so if your convention is not going to exceed 300 delegates, these three committees can be combined for greater efficiency.

Beyond the 300-delegate limit, it is wise to have the workload shared by as many people as possible. Print and Promotion could possibly be combined but maintain a separate Media Committee.

---

## PRINT COMMITTEE CHECKLIST

Review all print requirements □

Have each Conference Committee submit print
requirements □

List all requirements □

Cost estimate print requirements □

Design all necessary print material □

Obtain list of print suppliers and print houses □

Choose uniform typefaces, colors and design □

Prepare single tender and submit invitation bids □

Select printer from sealed bids □

Schedule receipt of all print material □

Deliver to committees as necessary □

Hire competent translators and interpreters □

Be fully responsible for final copy □

# 21

## Threading the
## SERVICES AND
## EQUIPMENT MAZE

**C**onfusion is guaranteed when convention committees independently requisition meeting rooms and make arrangements for materials and equipment for delivery heaven knows where, for use by heaven knows whom, for return heaven knows when. Unnecessary costs are incurred into the bargain.

How much simpler to create a Services and Equipment Committee. Make this group responsible for coordinating all public rooms, materials and supplies requests, receiving all conference aids, all rooms and equipment setups, as well as safekeeping and returning all equipment and supplies. In short, the chairman of this committee should be named as one of the hotel coordinators for the conference—authorized to negotiate and handle arrangements with hotel management personnel.

Eliminate chaos. Ten committee members, all negotiating with hotel representatives, are a sure sign of a major planning breakdown. Restrict hotel coordinators to four or less. Required are chairmen responsible for exhibits and displays, meals and refreshments, delegate accommodations and service and equipment. Some hotels prefer dealing with only one committee chairman. Check early to find which type of arrangement best suits your convention hotel.

Before anything happens at Services and Equipment planning sessions the committee must have a complete hotel inventory. Depending upon your particular convention requirements, necessary information to be obtained will probably include the following:

☐ Names of Hotel Manager, Assistant Managers, Maîtres D'Hôtel, Head Waiters, Engineer, Head Bellman, Security Chief, Other Department Managers.

☐ List of Hotel Rooms Available for Conference Events.

☐ Access Plan of All Event Rooms, Elevators, Stairs.

☐ Room Dimensions — Height, Length, Width.

☐ Flooring Alternatives available for all rooms — Carpet, Hardwood, Tile.

☐ Delegate Capacity All Rooms — Meeting Style, Dining Style, Reception Style.

☐ Number & Type of Head Table Platforms — Heights, Lengths, Widths, Seating Capacities.

☐ Number & Type of Conference Seating — Lengths, Widths, Comfort.

☐ Location, Size & Capacity of Coffee Break Areas.

☐ Location, Size & Capacity of Registration Areas.

☐ Location, Size & Capacity of Conference Office.

☐ Location, Size & Capacity of Media Facility.

☐ Location, Size and Capacity of Conference Storage Area.

☐ Evaluation of the Caliber of the Acoustics and Fire Proofing of Each Room.

☐ Detail — Electrical Services All Rooms, General Lighting and Locations, Lighting Controls and Locations, Electrical Outlets and Locations, Air Conditioning and Controls, Projection Booths and Locations, Window Locations and Blinds, Telephone Outlets and Locations, Interpretation Booths and Locations.

☐ Obtain Times Rooms are Available for Pre-Event Setup.

☐ Evaluate Hotel Public Address System: Clarity? Feedback? Built-In? Portable? Table, Lectern, Throat, Floor Mikes? Stand-by Sound Engineer? Background Music? Session Taping? Plug Ins?

☐ Evaluate Hotel Projection System: Movie Projectors? Slide Projectors? Screen Sizes? Locations? Screen Condition? Projection Brightness? Sound Clarity?

☐ Detail All Other Hotel Conference Equipment: Closed Circuit TV? Limousine Service? Copying and Duplicating Equipment? Easels? Chalkboards? Podiums? Lecterns? Spot and Flood Lights? Videotape Equipment?

☐ Determine Convention Site Safety: Precautions, Including Evacuation Procedures for Fires, Bomb Threats or Other Emergencies. Arrange 24-Hour Medical Service. Ask Your Hotel if They Offer This Facility.

Conference equipment today is almost human. Find out what is new and sophisticated and obtain informative literature on every possible piece of equipment which may be of a special use. Consult the convention center and hotel for advice on equipment.

Remember that you are acting on behalf of the other conference committees which may be too involved in developing their programs to thoroughly investigate all the conference aids. Special television equipment can bring the proceedings into every delegate's bedroom. Electronic pulse typewriters provide running-flow information on conference notice screens. Continuous-loop movie equipment is quite commonly used in exhibits and displays. Multiple-screen presentations are replacing single-screen shows. Chalkboards are almost as *passé* as buckboards.

Insist on excellence and efficiency. Convenience counts but not if the hotel equipment is inadequate or of a poor quality. If the available facilities are less than perfect, enter into contracts with outside convention supply houses rather than take a chance.

Good conference sound systems are an absolute essential. Insist on a sound system for every meeting room planned for 50 delegates or more. Recommended is a stereo system with amplifiers and separated speakers. Portable loudspeakers for large rooms should be avoided, as should oversize column speakers in small meeting areas. An inexpensive convention with a perfect sound system leaves delegates feeling that it was a million-dollar effort.

Call in the sound experts, tell them all your needs and have them bid for a total package contract. Require compatible components—microphones, taping, music and projectors should all plug into the one, single system. Insist, too, on continuous monitoring of all equipment.

Lapel mikes for speakers and lecturers allows them a freedom which can improve a convention immeasurably. Boom, whine, hiss, hum and feedback are easily eliminated distractions. Have the sound staff adjust all equipment before each event begins. Low amplification can be solved —rent good amplifiers.

Even though the perfect, pre-tested system is continuously monitored, never relax. Someone must be available—at the back of the room—to check volume and clarity at the start of every speech. Have the operator make the necessary adjustments. Speakers will be grateful and delegates will silently cheer.

Television cameras serve modern conferences effectively. Remote cameras are particularly useful in overflow situations. Pipe the video message into alternate rooms. Videotapes can be shown on large screens with a minimum of difficulty. Investigate two-way television station hookups for inter-city panel discussions.

Several cable television companies now specialize in conference services. An unused channel can broadcast—to locations chosen by you—a review of the previous day's major events, interviews, what's forthcoming or, if you want, the entire conference proceedings. Cable TV, closed-circuit style, is also an ideal information medium for news on local attractions and best restaurants. Moreover, multi-hookups are a must if delegates are housed in several hotels across the convention city.

Telephone companies across the continent offer conference calling services which allow delegates to talk with several people in different places at the same time. This communications technique can cut panel travel costs. Don't overlook any opportunity for saving—if you think conference calling has merit at your convention, contact your local telephone company. For example, the British Post Office in London, England began experimenting with Confravision service as early as 1971. Confravision introduced to several major U.K. centres the possibility of having two groups of five or so individuals, seated in studios, to carry on a two-way conversation, complete with visual and display facilities. Similarly, video conference calling in some Canadian and U.S. cities is available, through telephone companies, for small groups wanting to save staff time and travel.

Some conference committees tape the entire proceedings. This is a convenient permanent record which has added mileage as a source of revenue. Duplicate your master tapes and fill mail order requests from delegates and those unable to attend. Taping specialists can be called in to handle the job.

Thinking about slide or films? Projectors and screens must be located high enough off the convention floor so the projection beam is well above everyone's head. Super-size slide talks with lecturers standing in front of a 20-foot by 16-foot rear-projection screen are impressive and simple to set up. Whatever the size of the screen, chart, easel or chalk board it must be easily seen by everyone in the room. Good equipment should run silently but the further it is removed from delegates' ears, the better.

Two small reminders. Preview every film and slide presentation to make sure that the message is relevant, the presentation is goof-proof, and the image size is adequate. It's all part of expert projection technique to ensure that the impact comes from the program, rather than the equipment. In fact, all equipment must only be used to amplify messages, objectives or theme, unless the conference is a projection equipment trade show.

Think of the psychological factors inherent in every room situation. Seating well removed from the speaker or the projection screen, inhibits group discussion. Reduce mental barriers by lessening the physical distance! In large rooms set up speaker platforms on long walls, rather than end walls. In any event, place them on blank walls opposite entrance doors. Avoid 100-delegate audiences in rooms designed to seat 400 people.

Aisle widths are critical. Ensure ample space for delegate movement in and out of the meeting hall as well as space for audience mikes. Be prepared for protest-type demonstrations as well. Hire security staff who have been sensitively and sensibly trained to handle these situations. Prompt and inconspicuous action is needed to remove the unruly. Protests are on the increase. Meet with Program Group Committees to develop a policy which will enable all to stick to the agenda and channel protest into general discussion periods.

And you may have to provide security for some VIP guests. It is now quite common to be involved in these assignments, particularly when senior government representatives are scheduled as featured conference speakers. Most have their own security detail and you can expect to be contacted. Be prepared, too, for such requests as security rooms on either side of the VIP suite, private elevator facilities and permission to examine any rooms the VIP will occupy. Above all, access throughout the hotel will be reviewed and a policy established to get the dignitary through the crowds. Play it safe even if the VIP has no personal security detail.

Several other items concern the Services Committee. Stage and platform design can be a despair. High platforms in small meeting rooms create psychological barriers. Low platforms in large auditoriums mean delegates can't see what is going on. The length of every head-table platform is critical. Significantly, the fewer head-table guests, the more positive the group and its aims. Ideal table length is 30 inches per person.

Sunlight windows are fine for a breakfast event but are not appropriate for speech and work sessions. There's nothing more distracting than trying to concentrate on a presentation when the speaker or panelists are seated in front of a brilliant window wall. In such situations ensure that there are drapes or window shades which will shut out light when required.

Like most conference details, there is a method to the planning of the room arrangements for every event. Some of the many layouts are:

AUDITORIUM SETUPS: Events exceeding 300 persons in a meeting situation or 200 people at a dinner event.

| | |
|---|---|
| Classroom Style | Schoolroom Style |
| Hot Seat Style | Tier Style |
| Luncheon Style | Theatre Style |
| Reception Style | "V" Style |

MEETING ROOM SETUPS: Sessions scheduled for less than 300 persons per meeting or less than 200 delegates at a dinner event.

| | |
|---|---|
| Director's Style | Rap Style |
| Hollow Square | Reception Style |
| Horizontal Style | Schoolroom Style |
| Horseshoe Style | Vertical Style |
| Newsroom Style | Tier Style |
| | "U" Style |

To determine which arrangement best suits your purposes analyze each event in relation to the available meeting rooms. Consider the following factors:

> Number of delegates attending the event
> Type of meeting taking place
> Audiovisual equipment requirements
> Presentation method to be used

Design special setups for speaker sessions, reception areas, media centre, office and storage rooms. Be prepared to provide emergency services. You will need to obtain first-aid supplies, insecticides and tools. Don't overlook anything. Have a supply of miscellaneous items on hand — paper clips, pens, pencils, extension cords, notebooks, typewriter ribbons, duplicating paper and the like.

Supervise each conference room setup undertaken by the hotel staff. Everything must be in place 15 minutes before any function begins. Monitor all equipment, including lighting, heating and air conditioning controls. Make sure drapes and window blinds open and close at scheduled times. When the conference is over ensure that borrowed equipment is returned promptly to each owner, along with a written thank-you letter.

The sample contract below can be modified for almost any conference supply situation.

THE NORTH AMERICAN PROMOTIONS
ASSOCIATION ANNUAL CONVENTION
BENSON BAY HOTEL, LANDMARK

JULY 9, 10, 11, 12, 19—

TENDER: PUBLIC ADDRESS SYSTEM

We the ................................, as CONTRACTOR, do

hereby tender the following price $............. as total cost estimate to provide a complete public address system with compatible taping and music service for The North American Promotions Association Annual Convention, as the ASSOCIATION.

We acknowledge payment will be made by the ASSOCIATION within 30 (thirty) days after completion of the Annual Convention.

It is understood we, as CONTRACTOR, must coordinate all sound system requirements, installation and removal with the Electrician, BENSON BAY HOTEL, and the Chairman, SERVICES AND EQUIPMENT COMMITTEE, of the ASSOCIATION.

Both the HOTEL and the ASSOCIATION are saved harmless from any accident, loss or theft to the CONTRACTOR'S equipment and services. The CONTRACTOR acknowledges his responsibility to provide equipment as listed 15 minutes before each conference session and event and to provide continuous monitoring of all equipment during each convention session and event.

The equipment will operate in good working condition without over or under-amplification and substitute equipment will be immediately available on failure of any equipment or parts originally supplied by the CONTRACTOR.

IN WITNESS WHEREOF the parties hereto have executed and agreed to these presents and the terms and conditions hereunder noted.

Approved this .......... day of  NORTH AMERICAN
.................. 19—. Receipt   PROMOTIONS ASSOCIATION
of $............. acknowledged  ........................
as 10 per cent of the tender bid.  SERVICES AND EQUIPMENT
                                   CHAIRMAN

.........................     ........................
        WITNESS                      CONTRACTOR

TERMS AND CONDITIONS
SOUND EQUIPMENT REQUIREMENTS

TUESDAY, JULY 8

7:30 p.m. - 9:30 p.m.: Hunt Room, Second Floor
Supply and install one stereo music system, (cartridge or cassette only) two speakers, separate tone, balance controls, 30-foot separation between speakers. Supply three hours minimum cartridge or cassette music — rock, contemporary, mood — minimum of voice. Plus one floor mike spliced into system *or* alternate sound system. This unit to be monitored by operator supplied by sound company.

WEDNESDAY, JULY 9

8:00 a.m. - 9:30 a.m.: Crystal Ball Room, Second Floor
Stereo system and taped music as above, 50-foot separation between speakers. Contemporary music, no voice — one hour minimum. Plus one floor mike spliced into system *or* alternate sound system. This unit to be monitored by operator provided by sound company.

12:00 noon - 12:30 p.m.: Exhibit Lounge, Second Floor
One floor mike and sound system monitored by sound company operator.

12:30 p.m. - 1:45 p.m.: Crystal Ball Room, Second Floor
One table mike at head table and sound system monitored by sound company operator.

2:30 p.m. - 5:00 p.m.: Second Floor
Four three-table mikes and four audience mikes sound systems and operator. Two systems to be located in Crystal Ball Room, one in Hunt Room, one in Exhibit Lounge.

6:30 p.m. - 8:30 p.m.: Crystal Ball Room, Second Floor
Two head table mikes, sound system and operator in Ball Room.
9:00 p.m. - 10:30 p.m.: Exhibit Lounge, Second Floor
One floor mike located at MacNeil Booth entrance and sound system monitored by sound company operator.

THURSDAY, JULY 10

7:30 a.m. - 9:00 a.m.: Logan Room, Main Floor
Same equipment and operator as per 8:00 a.m. — 9:30 a.m. Wed., July 9, in Crystal Ball Room, Second Floor. Music to be of different variety than that of Wednesday.
9:00 a.m. - 2:00 p.m.: Lemoine Park Zoo
Provide two long-range portable loud hailers for Family Group Committee.
9:00 a.m. - 12:00 noon: Crystal Ball Room, Second Floor
Seven table mikes, six audience mikes and sound system plus tape equipment built into system for recording. Five hours of tape to be supplied. Operator to monitor this system continuously and tape all proceedings.
12:30 p.m. - 2:15 p.m.: La Blanche Room, Mezzanine Floor
One head table mike, one floor mike at end of head table, sound system and operator to monitor system continuously.
2:30 p.m. - 5:00 p.m.: Second Floor
Four three-table mikes and four audience mikes, sound system set up as per 2:30 p.m. - 5:00 p.m., Wed., July 9, plus tape recording equipment. Operator to monitor continuously and tape all proceedings.
5:30 p.m. - 6:30 p.m.: Crystal Ball Room, Second Floor
One floor mike at center of room, sound system and operator.
7:00 p.m. - 9:00 p.m.: Logan Room, Main Floor
Three head table mikes, sound system and operator. Operator to monitor system continuously.

FRIDAY, JULY 11

7:00 a.m. - 3:00 p.m.: Landmark Star Cruise
Two long-range portable loud hailers for Family Group Committee.
6:00 p.m. - 7:00 p.m.: Logan Room, Main Floor
Supply taped music entertainment — no mikes. Contemporary music, no voice — one hour minimum.
7:00 p.m. - 9:15 p.m.: La Blanche Room, Mezzanine Floor
Supply and monitor one table mike, one floor mike and sound system.

SATURDAY, JULY 12

9:00 a.m. - 11:00 a.m.: Washington Room, Mezzanine Floor
Supply and monitor two floor mikes, taped music and sound system.
9:00 a.m. - 11:00 a.m.: Hunt Room, Second Floor
Supply and monitor same as to 9:00 a.m. - 11:00 a.m., Sat., July

11, Washington Room. (One operator cannot monitor both systems at the same time.)

DATED THIS ......... DAY OF ....................... 19.....

...................................
CONTRACTOR

---

## SERVICES & EQUIPMENT COMMITTEE CHECKLIST

Complete and detailed list of all service, material and
  equipment requirements ☐
Evaluate hotel inventory ☐
Evaluate all modern conference aids ☐
Review all services and material requirements ☐
Suggest improvements or alternatives ☐
Contact conference suppliers ☐
Evaluate supplier's equipment, staff and reputation ☐
Prepare services and materials tenders ☐
Coordinate all session and event room requirements ☐
Suggest improvements or alternatives ☐
Diagram each meeting and event room ☐
Set up each meeting and event room ☐
Supply all services and equipment ☐
Return all equipment immediately if no further use
  is contemplated ☐
Pass proceedings and tapes to Post-Conference Committee ☐

Examples of some typical conference room seating arrangements. For large groups use auditorium-style seating. Ask your hotel or convention facility about other room plans.

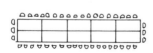

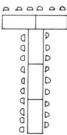

For small rooms and small groups use the board room or T-shape seating plans.

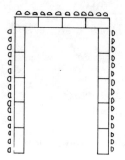 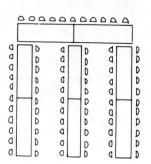

To bring delegates closer together you may wish to use the U- or E-shape arrangement.

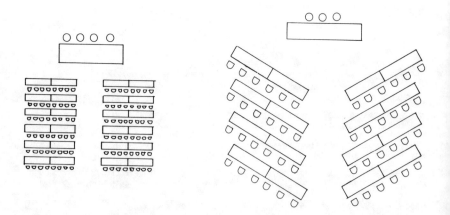

One of these classroom arrangements is particularly useful when delegates need to take notes.

# 22

## Getting from A to B –
# TRANSPORTATION TACTICS

**C**an 600 delegates — registered in two hotels — feel totally a part of a conference that has plenary sessions in an auditorium, work sessions in both hotels, receptions and displays in an outside hall and some banquets in another?

The situation described is typical of today's conference and gives some indication of the planning problems which face the Transportation Committee.

Transit requirements for most conferences — even the 250 to 600 delegate variety — are such that the Transportation Committee should be on its own to handle the necessary arrangements. Services and equipment is largely an internal operation, transportation is an external matter. It is almost impossible for a single committee to manage these two operations.

If delegates have to stay in more than one hotel, plan and organize an inter-hotel transit system. This will minimize weather problems, increase delegate attendance and reduce delegate transportation costs. A safe bet is to hire a transit company to provide service for your early and late arrivals. Buses should be running 30 minutes before the first conference event and terminate 30 minutes after the final session. Route maps, outlining the scheduled trips between hotels and session sites are necessary. Put a copy in each delegate's kit and have extra maps available at the information desk and on the buses.

Conference tours are appreciated when planned with delegates in mind. Busing delegates to out-of-hotel sessions provides an excellent opportunity for sightseeing and commentary on local points-of-interest. Tours are most successful when they are short and include stops and walks. Bull horns or public address systems may be necessary and good tight scripting is also essential. Above all have interpreters on hand for foreign delegates.

For a total change consider boat cruises down major rivers or along the waterfront. There is an added educational bonus in such events — script them to include interesting historical data and commentary on major highlights. Perhaps this is the one out-of-hotel event. If so, tie it in with an all-delegate shipboard meal. Refreshments and food are usually required fare on cruises so kill two birds with one stone.

No matter what mode of transportation is used all vehicles must be on time. If mass transit is involved keep track of everyone by taking head counts every time the group boards the buses. Save one bus for the stragglers who consistently seem to be five minutes late.

Mass transit costs per delegate are fairly standard across North America. But beware, some equipment may come from the ox-cart era. Bear in mind that transit companies are constantly purchasing new equipment — insist on their newest and most modern vehicles with built-in public address systems. The committee must pre-drive every route to reduce travel time. Routes and time of day must be planned to avoid high temperatures and traffic jams.

Chauffeured transportation costs money but is always preferable to committee-car service. Also, committee workers want to attend as many conference events as possible. When they are chauffeuring major speakers to media interviews they are out of the convention picture. This simply means rent transportation whenever possible. Committee workers can provide standby cars for emergencies but this should really be the limit. Remember, too, news releases require immediate delivery to media absent from the convention sessions. Hire taxis for this.

The Transportation Committee is the transit adviser to all other conference committees. Be able to suggest what can be done, how much time is required and anticipated costs. If you discover something unique and interesting — a dune buggy rental service on a beautiful sandy beach or a snowmobile rental company at a state or national park — then recommend it. Insurance requirements must be met so make sure Finance has included transportation coverage in the total convention insurance package.

While planning the Transportation Committee operation, remember to have conference first-aid kits and insecticides on hand. Prepare a list with the names and addresses of the nearest available ambulances, doctors, clinics and hospitals for out-of-hotel events. Lay on standby cars to provide emergency transportation. Putting it bluntly, the Transportation Committee is responsible for all delegates when they are away from the conference headquarters at any convention-sponsored event. The sample contract below may be of assistance to this Committee.

THE NORTH AMERICAN PROMOTIONS
ASSOCIATION ANNUAL CONVENTION
BENSON BAY HOTEL, LANDMARK

JULY 9, 10, 11, 12, 19—

TENDER: TRANSIT SERVICES

We, the .................................., as CONTRACTOR do hereby tender the following price of $............. as total cost estimate to provide a total transit system, air conditioned equipment and public address equipment, together with bonded transit drivers, for the NORTH AMERICAN PROMOTIONS ASSOCIATION ANNUAL CONFERENCE, as ASSOCIATION.

We acknowledge payment will be made by the ASSOCIATION within 30 (thirty) days after completion of the ANNUAL CONVENTION.

It is understood we, as CONTRACTOR, must coordinate all transit requirements with the chairman, TRANSPORTATION COMMITTEE, NORTH AMERICAN PROMOTIONS ASSOCIATION.

THE ASSOCIATION is saved harmless from any accident to its delegates or from any accident, loss or theft to the CONTRACTOR'S equipment and services. The CONTRACTOR acknowledges his responsibility to provide all equipment as listed five minutes before each conference session and event and to have substitute equipment immediately available on failure of any equipment or parts originally supplied by the CONTRACTOR.

ON WITNESS WHEREOF the parties hereto have executed and agreed to these presents and the terms and conditions hereunder noted:

Approved this .......... day of      THE NORTH AMERICAN

............... 19..... Receipt      PROMOTIONS ASSOCIATION

of $............. acknowledged      ........................
as 10 per cent deposit of the ten-      TRANSPORTATION
der bid.      CHAIRMAN

........................      ........................
    WITNESS            CONTRACTOR

TERMS AND CONDITIONS
TRANSIT EQUIPMENT REQUIREMENTS

TUESDAY, JULY 8, 19 —

10:00 a.m. - Provide one 40-passenger, air-conditioned bus BENSON BAY HOTEL AND LA GRANDE HOTEL to transport delegates to FORT BENSON HOTEL for early arrivals function.

WEDNESDAY, JULY 9, 19 —

9:30 a.m. - 11:30 a.m. Provide two, 40-passenger, air-conditioned buses. Buses to be reduced to one bus only between the following hours 9:00 a.m. - 11:30 a.m., 2:00 p.m. - 4:30 p.m., 7:00 p.m. - 10:30 p.m.

8:00 a.m. - Pick up two speakers, FLIGHT 905, LANDMARK INTERNATIONAL AIRPORT, deliver to BENSON BAY HOTEL.

11:00 a.m. - Pick up two speakers, FLIGHT 831, deliver to BENSON BAY HOTEL. (All flight pick ups at Landmark International Airport.)

9:00 p.m. - Deliver one speaker to FLIGHT 733. Pick up at LA GRANDE HOTEL.

THURSDAY, JULY 10, 19 —

7:00 a.m. - 10:00 p.m. Provide two 40-passenger air-conditioned buses as above on Wed., July 9, 19—. Buses to be reduced to one bus only between the following hours 9:00 a.m. - 11:30 a.m., 3:00 p.m. - 4:30 p.m., 6:30 p.m. - 8:00 p.m.

9:00 a.m. - 2:00 p.m. Provide three 40-passenger air-conditioned buses for civic park and zoo tour. Public address system and washroom required on each bus. Pick up and return to FORT BENSON HOTEL along following route: West on Broadway, south on George, west on Wildwood, south on Main, east on Kenmore, south on Logan to park. From Park north on Avenue of Americas, east on Logan, north on Sycamore, east on Merchant, through Market Square, west on Ralph, north on George, west on Broadway to BENSON BAY HOTEL.

9:15 a.m. - Pick up one speaker FLIGHT 915, deliver to BENSON BAY HOTEL.

9:45 a.m. - Deliver three speakers FLIGHT 988, pick up LA GRANDE HOTEL.
Pick up two speakers, FLIGHT 988, deliver to BENSON BAY HOTEL.

11:00 a.m. - Pick up one speaker, FLIGHT 831, deliver to BENSON BAY HOTEL.

3:00 p.m. - Deliver three speakers to FLIGHT 614, from LA GRANDE.

11:30 p.m.  -  Pick up two speakers, FLIGHT 137, deliver to BENSON BAY HOTEL.

FRIDAY, JULY 11, 19 —

7:00 a.m.  -  8:00 a.m. Provide six, 40-passenger, air-conditioned buses for LANDMARK Cruise. Public address system and washroom required in each bus. Four-bus pick up at BENSON BAY HOTEL, and two-bus pick up at LA GRANDE HOTEL. LA GRANDE buses to proceed direct to BENSON BAY HOTEL, no stop and then follow route: west on Broadway, north on Main, east on Portage, north on St. Mary's, east on Bank to Cruise dock. Buses return to garage.

1:30 a.m.  -  3:00 p.m. Provide six, 40-passenger buses as above on Friday, July 11, at 7:00 a.m. - 8:00 a.m. Six bus pick up at Fort Heritage. South on Highway 12, west on Highway 10 to AGRICULTURAL SITE. Return to city at 2:00 p.m., east on Highway 10, South on Highway 12, south on Main, west on Portage, south on Portage, south on Smith, west on Broadway to HOTEL. Two buses continue to LA GRANDE HOTEL.

3:00 p.m.  -  Deliver three speakers to FLIGHT 614, pick up, LA GRANDE HOTEL.

DATED THIS . . . . . . . . . day of . . . . . . . . . . . . . . . . . . . . . . . . 19. . . .

. . . . . . . . . . . . . . . . . . . . . . . . . . . . . . . . . . . .
CONTRACTOR

---

## TRANSPORTATION COMMITTEE CHECKLIST

|   |   |
|---|---|
| Survey all transportation requirements | ☐ |
| Evaluate all transportation services | ☐ |
| Coordinate information with all committees | ☐ |
| Review all transportation requests | ☐ |
| Suggest improvements | ☐ |
| Evaluate transit equipment and staff | ☐ |
| Prepare transit tenders | ☐ |
| Establish cost estimates | ☐ |
| Have emergency cars on hand | ☐ |
| Provide taxi delivery service as necessary | ☐ |
| Check parking facilities at hotel and out-of-hotel locations | ☐ |
| Assign group leaders for all mass transportation | ☐ |

# 23

## Rational Approaches to
## REGISTRATION
## AND INFORMATION

**A** cheerful and warm welcome for every delegate sets the convention tone. Personable registration staff can do it all — put your best foot forward here and delegates will be pleasantly and positively impressed.

Confusion and chaos are unsatisfactory greetings for weary travellers. What is needed is an efficient and sparkling Registration and Information Committee in a setting that is intimate yet large enough to handle several delegates at one time. Here everything happens like clockwork, and delegates are provided with pertinent information from dawn to dusk, quickly and courteously. A solitary cloth-covered table in a noisy, cramped corner will not do.

All registrants' questions — and there will be many — should be handled at a separate Information Desk. Registration staff must be helpful, well informed and polite, yet able to direct questioners to the information area, so the registration process continues uninterrupted.

Advance or pre-registration systems are a godsend to delegates and Registration Committees alike. Insist on it during Finance Committee planning discussions and give discounts for early registration. Advance payments mean money earning interest for the conference well before it begins. Apart from that it saves every delegate time because registration forms have been processed well before their arrival.

Conferences convened for more than 400 delegates have no alternative. A system must be designed to ensure at least 80 per cent pre-registration. Conference kits containing all material can be distributed quickly to most delegates upon presentation of the registration receipt, while the remaining 20 per cent are processed speedily and efficiently.

In fact, pre-registration should be considered for all conferences, congresses and conventions. Hotels require detailed hotel reservations several months in advance from all delegates — so why not follow the same policy. Chapter 24 details reservation hints. Suffice to say here, pre-register as many delegates as possible.

Registration Centers have to open in advance — at least a day or two before the conference begins. It is surprising how many delegates arrive before the official opening and are interested in knowing who else is coming. Processing local delegates early also cuts down the registration crush. If local registration exceeds 200, consider a separate advance registration day for in-town delegates, perhaps one week before the conference.

You can determine when to open the Registration Center by checking delegate arrival times indicated on their registration forms. Open up each day 30 minutes before the first event and close 30 minutes before the final session. Reduce workloads and costs by limited staffing or shutting down during dinner hours. As soon as the majority of delegates are registered, shift the operation to the Information Center.

Sooner or later, some committee member suggests separate registration desks for different attendant categories: delegates, observers, affiliates, university members, spouses, children and VIP's. It is a bad idea. Every registrant deserves equal treatment. Besides, families like to make decisions when they are all together.

A free-flow registration system guarantees registration sanity when everyone else is going mad. Free-flow is a series of progressing registration stations with separated functions arranged in proper sequence.

A good free-flow system contains one continuous row of individual stations such as:

> RECEIPTS STATION — receipts for late or partial fees, exchanges on events tickets, sells tickets for guests, refunds where necessary. Staffed by Finance Committee, backed up by Information Center and Accommodation personnel.
> DOCUMENTATION STATION — completion of registration forms and distribution of conference badges for late registrants. Staffed by Registration Committee, supported by Information Center and Accommodation personnel.

REGISTRATION STATION — check off all delegates for maintenance and duplication of delegate roster. Staffed by Registration Committee.

MATERIALS STATION — distribution of pre-prepared delegates' kits. Kits bear individual names and are filed in alphabetical order. Also distribute similar kits to late registrants. Registration Committee staffing.

PARTIAL EVENTS STATION — special service station for those who want to attend certain events, one or two days, or want to bring friends. Fill out a form, take it to the Receipts Station, pay the required amount and pick up the necessary tickets. Staffed by Registration Committee.

LOCAL EVENTS STATION — distribution of non-conference literature or where-to-buy-and-eat. Include tours, opera, ballet, musicals, nightclubs, festivals, art galleries and anniversary celebration events. Travel bureaus, box-office agents will often supply staff for this station. Payment for these events is handled on a cash basis.

INFORMATION CENTER — the place for personal or individual questions and instant responses. Delegate refunds, lost items, complimentary registrations, last minute reservations and changes all are handled here. Select trained personnel who will be able to handle inquiries of this nature. Draw up policies covering all situations. Manned by Registration and Accommodation Committee Chairmen.

Preferably the Information Center will be located immediately adjacent to the Registration Area. The room can then be utilized for all conference office requirements, particularly Finance, Services and Equipment, Transportation, Events, Hosting and Administration. In any event, locate direct, outside-line telephones here but restrict their use to conference staff.

Concentrate on speeding up the registration process. Role-play training works wonders. Time 20 "delegates" through the system and have the staff tighten up procedures. Every second saved improves delegate attitudes.

If the Registration Committee expects to manage an effective registration system keep the following points in mind:

Ask delegates questions that require a yes or no answer
Eliminate as much typing and writing as possible
Hire well-trained registration personnel
Move registrants through a single line
Label each registration station
Ask for written hotel guarantee to adequately staff hotel registration desk and bellman's station when the majority of delegates are scheduled to arrive

The registration speed-up process actually begins several months prior to the opening date with the design of the conference registration form. Save time and energy by deciding on a multiple-copy, self-carbon form.

One copy is needed by Registration, one by Finance, and one for the convention hotel. A fourth copy is necessary for receipt and acknowledgment purposes. A fifth copy may be required if registration processing is undertaken by the organization's national office. Registration forms should be printed on self-carbon continuous forms in the conference colors, bear the conference logo and have adequate space for writing or typing.

Very little information is requested on good registration forms — and people usually fill them out by hand. Ask for short replies only.

> Address and full name required for delegate's badge
> Affiliation or membership status
> Attending spouse's name
> Children's names and ages — if it is a family conference
> Registration fee and room rates
> Receipt acknowledgment
> Babysitting requirements
> Transportation mode, date and time of arrival and departure

Accommodation descriptions are seldom included on registration forms today as most hotels provide sufficient complimentary forms — developed over several years in the business. Use them, it will save you money.

The registration and hotel accommodation forms are mailed together to prospective delegates by the Registration Committee for return to the Finance Committee. Finance arranges receipts, returns one registration form to the delegate and retains the second copy for record purposes. Copy three and the hotel accommodation form goes to Accommodation which matches room requests to known hotel rooms. Then, these two forms are handed to the hotel management as soon as possible. Finance passes the fourth copy on to Registration which draws up the delegate roster, completes conference badges and kits and advises all committees of the anticipated number of delegates.

Shown here is a sample of an effective, multiple, self-carbon registration form.

## REGISTRATION COMMITTEE CHECKLIST

Select registration desk locale ☐
Analyze registration systems ☐
Determine required facilities and equipment ☐
Prepare facilities and equipment tenders ☐
Order furniture from Services Committee ☐
Order telephones from Services Committee ☐
Order signs, notices from Printing Committee ☐
Prepare draft registration procedures ☐

## REGISTRATION FORM

## THE NORTH AMERICAN PROMOTIONS ASSOCIATION ANNUAL CONFERENCE
### Benson Bay Hotel, Landmark — July 9, 10, 11, 12, 19—.

### APPLICATION FOR REGISTRATION

Mail this application together with room reservation request and registration cheque to: **Finance Chairman, PROMOTION IN THE 80s, P.O. Box 111, Landmark.**

### REGISTRATION FEES

| | | | |
|---|---|---|---|
| Delegate Members | $50 | Spouse of Member | $25 |
| Non-members | $65 | Spouse of Non-member | $30 |
| Single day fee | $20 | Child | $15 |

All Sessions, Receptions and Three Meals a day are provided with payment of these fees. DEADLINE FOR GUARANTEED ACCOMMODATIONS IS APRIL, 10, 19—. Confirmation and other details regarding accommodation will be handled by the Benson Bay Hotel, Landmark.

### FOR CONFERENCE OFFICE USE

Receipt of $............. in Registration Fees acknowledged as of ............. 19.........

............. Finance Chairman.

Delegate's Name ............................................... (include preferred first name or nickname)

Spouse's Name ...............................................

Children's Names ............................................... Age.........
............................................... Age.........
............................................... Age.........

Business Address ...............................................

Home Address ...............................................

ARRIVAL — Time......... Date......... Via.........

DEPARTURE — Time......... Date......... Via.........

Baby sitter services required ☐ Yes ☐ No

Select registration personnel ☐
Consider professional registration company ☐
Determine personnel job duties ☐
Establish staff work schedules ☐
Develop Questions/Answers list for staff ☐
Train registration and information staff ☐
Pre-register as many delegates as possible ☐
Coordinate registrations with reservations ☐
Complete registration procedures ☐
Maintain registration lists by hotel room number ☐
Establish refunds policy ☐
Determine adequate cash control ☐
Establish cheque and credit policy ☐
Determine security and accounting procedures ☐
Develop ticket sales policy ☐
Maintain ticket sales controls ☐
Receive all delegates kit material ☐
Fill kits — name badges, programs, meal and event
   tickets, general information ☐
Distribute all delegate kits ☐
Develop message distribution system ☐
Handle all conference and delegate messages ☐
Acquire and distribute tourist information ☐
Confirm out-of-conference bookings ☐
Obtain church service information ☐
Develop VIP welcome policy ☐
Prepare community events brochure ☐
Prepare community entertainment and buyer's guide ☐
Arrange for interpreters and translation equipment ☐

The Perils of
# BED, BOARD
# AND HOSTING

**T**hink of your delegates as guests in your own home and you will appreciate that it is not in good taste to leave all arrangements in the hands of the hotel management. Moreover, good hosts never assume that guests can fully attend to their own needs once they are settled in.

Clearly, it is the responsibility of the Accommodation Committee to develop and manage a good hotel liaison program. The committee must also be prepared to attend to last minute room requirements and resolve problems such as late-night parties. In addition, conference staff have to be on hand to minister to the needs of the association's VIP's, speakers and special guests.

The more problems anticipated in advance and the more names of hotel contacts committed to paper, the smoother delegate arrangements will be. What you are striving for is a plan which allows the hotel's guest facilities and services to be used to best advantage by every delegate. Moreover, these findings have to be communicated clearly to the Registration Committee because both groups must work very closely together.

What does the Accommodation Committee have to know? A wide range of items really, all very important in detailed accommodation planning. Discuss the following points in depth with the hotel reservations manager:

How many single and double rooms are available? How many have connecting doors? Will these rooms accommodate extra beds, cribs or cots? These rooms are usually assigned to regular speakers, panelists and delegates. Save the largest inexpensive rooms for families with small children.

How many bed-sitting rooms are available? What sizes are involved? Large ones are excellent for small meetings and low-profile hospitality suites.

How many regular one-bedroom suites are available? These will be required for local association presidents or chairmen and national committee executives and key speakers.

How many VIP suites are available? These suites, usually containing two or more bedrooms and a sitting room, are assigned to senior national and local executives or heads of state. The national president gets the best. The incoming chairman, or president rates equal or choice. Check to see if they wish to share a suite.

How many hospitality suites are available? On what floors are they located? Hospitality suites are least objectionable when located next to elevators.

What are the guaranteed room rates and appointments for every class of room? Remember to get a firm written commitment of what the rates will be during convention week.

Obtain names and telephone numbers of hotel staff who directly control room allocations — shift by shift.

Meet the hotel staff members who ultimately settle major snags: the manager, assistant managers, night managers — again shift by shift.

Inspect every room type and rate each accordingly to acceptability. Check for size, air-conditioning, bath, floor location, radio and television, proximity to elevators. Most rooms are similar if located in the same spot on each floor. However, ensure furniture age, condition and quality are the same in similar rooms. Hotels often have renovation programs under way and the rooms you previewed may be the "after" not the "before" version.

It's important that each delegate has similar accommodation and appointments, but this is rarely possible. So in matching delegates to rooms, do your best to minimize potential friction.

As soon as the conference hotel is named, be on guard for the one or two early birds who will immediately reserve the best rooms on VIP floors. The president could end up sleeping in the linen closet next to the freight elevator! Circumvent this by pre-reserving sufficient special purpose rooms several months before the conference begins.

Know how hospitality suites should work and be controlled. Set opening and closing hours. Investigate state, provincial and local liquor laws and their application. Check to see that each sponsor has made a complete and full agreement with the hotel catering manager for all room and service charges. Prepare a list of the officials who will be in charge of each hospitality suite.

Hospitality suites function best when they are only one floor away from the prime action areas. Book one hospitality suite early for the sponsors of next year's convention. They may ask for this type of accommodation at the last moment.

A large VIP suite should be reserved for the Conference Committee as close to the convention floor as possible. About a five-room, three bathroom setup is the best. It will provide meeting, hospitality and change rooms in addition to separate bedrooms for the conference chairman and co-chairman at minimum cost. Local delegates and committee members need a place to freshen up and change. This can be the spot for it.

Tell local delegates and staff about the committee facility. The meeting and hospitality room will serve other purposes such as speaker receptions, committee meetings and meetings of the full committee staff. But this is not the place for the conference office.

Avoid the impulse to overbook hotel rooms. If 300 rooms are requested, you will probably discover the hotel has allocated 315 rooms — a five per cent margin. Hotels usually check amongst themselves to determine the previous conference attendance to avoid embarrassments. Even at the formal reservation cut-off date, most hotels will hold a few rooms in reserve. Check early with the convention hotel management to find out what their room booking policy is, particularly if there will be another conference in the hotel.

The Accommodation Committee must instruct hotel accounting staff on charges emanating from all rooms which will be paid out of conference funds. Usually, speakers and other special guests expect you to pay for rooms plus laundry, valet and meal service. Long-distance telephone charges and refreshments are normally the responsibility of the room occupant, unless the sky is the expense limit. Negotiate these arrangements with the Speakers Committee so VIP speakers and lecturers know conference limitations.

Accommodation Committees have to be on the ball early with a host of information at their fingertips. They operate out of the Registration Area, usually staffing the Information Center in tandem with the Registration Committee. Expect questions on food service, bar service hours,

# SUCCESSFUL CONFERENCE & CONVENTION PLANNING

room service, baby-sitting, hair stylists, costume rentals, hotel entertainment as well as local attractions including entertainment, restaurants and sports events. Develop a fact sheet which covers these items as a quick reference.

Effective Accommodation Committees include one or more Hosting Teams. This added touch requires outgoing individuals who are assigned to special conference guest speakers. Remember VIP expenses are more commonly borne by employers than by the conference coffers. It is these VIPs who particularly deserve automatic and courteous attention from Hosting Teams.

The moment special guests indicate they will attend the conference, assign hosts and hostesses. Advise all such guests by letter of the host or hostesses' name and address, mentioning that they will be available to provide assistance and information during the conference.

Prudence counts of course. Overeager hosts can fence VIPs in. An instinctive knowledge of the particular VIP's requirements is essential and function accordingly.

Hosting Team service covers everything from local transportation, arrival and departure pickups, shopping trips, arrangements for non-conference meetings to revising travel or accommodation.

Hosts should be flexible. During a recent airline strike one host volunteered to drive his VIP some 300 miles across an international border to the nearest operating airport. The VIP was able to make alternate connections to get to his next meeting. When the host's employer learned what had happened, he underwrote the expenses involved.

Accommodation Committee members need to know what every committee is doing and what is happening at every conference event. They also have to be tuned into the best local attractions and be able to provide special transportation when necessary. As well, the committee has to ensure that every VIP, speaker and lecturer attends each event at which they are to be featured guests.

---

## ACCOMMODATION COMMITTEE CHECKLIST

Coordinate all activity with Registration Committee ☐
Develop formal hotel liaison agreement ☐
Establish accommodation and complaints policy ☐
Host VIP members, speakers and guests ☐
Complete hotel room survey ☐
Allocate hotel rooms according to accommodation policy ☐
Develop hospitality suite policy ☐
Instruct hotel not to accept any suite reservations
    directly from delegates ☐

Operate convention staff suite ☐
Advise convention staff of suite particulars ☐
Advise local delegates of suite particulars ☐
Select information staff ☐
Develop fact sheet with Registration Committee ☐
Train all accommodation staff ☐
Dry-run accommodation and information systems ☐
Establish staff work schedules ☐

# 25

## The Substance of
# MEETING MEDIA NEEDS

t is generally expected that a conference or convention should be newsworthy and generate some immediate, dramatic comment and public awareness, both favorable and constructive. If media coverage at the previous conference was a letdown — bet on lapses in conference planning — rather than disinterest on the part of the media.

Certainly, most Media Committees do realize they must assist the media. All too often though, the job is not done in a professional manner. Start with commonsense basics. Short of the president absconding with the association funds, the conference is the biggest association news event of the year. Let the media know that major and meaningful speakers will attend and that worthwhile sessions are in the offing.

At the preliminary planning stages establish a clear media policy and stick with it. The trick is to get the organization and conference message to the general public. This is not to imply all trade secrets must be public knowledge. Rather, the plan is to get accurate, unbiased coverage of the convention to local, national and international audiences.

And remember it's the media, not the press. Similarly, it is a news room, not a press room. Media organizations include international and national wire and cable services, local and network radio and television stations, business and trade journals, weekly newspapers, the national financial press and local dailies, as well as association publications.

The largest newspapers may have news specialists for every conceivable situation, while small weeklies often consist of one owner doubling as a news reporter. Every reporter can't be an instant expert on every conference. No single media outlet will cover regular conventions with a battery of news and feature reporters. In fact, media coverage will be minimal unless all outlets are well-informed — in advance — of what your conference has to offer in themes and speakers.

Think of each major outlet as having news reporters, feature writers, editorial writers, financial reporters, political reporters, sports reporters, lifestyle reporters and entertainment writers, to name a few. The job of the Media Committee is to determine what conference items will appeal to each. A word to the wise — newspapers now have family or lifestyle sections in lieu of women's pages.

Good media representation today means ensuring the Media Committee room has a high degree of sophistication, is fully equipped and is located on the convention floor. Inform the media of your location — and your facilities. In major cities where the competition for news coverage is intense, set up a five-section facility with areas for news conferences, news visuals, news lounge, news room and duplicating room. This type of arrangement provides a comfortable working environment which will keep your media representatives on hand. For smaller conventions, one area will be sufficient, provided there is ample space for getting out the news.

In any event, be frank and open with the media, not hesitant or superior. The arrangement suggested here can benefit your association and the media:

> NEWS CONFERENCE ROOM — where all major stories are revealed and VIP executives and speakers meet the media. Head table with two or three chairs, a good visual backdrop, mikes and taping equipment and sufficient chairs — classroom style. Pencils, paper and ashtrays are also required.
> NEWS VISUALS ROOM — where VIPs, executives and speakers can be photographed and televised. Lounge-style with sofas, chairs and drapes, mikes, television, video taping, cable TV and photographic equipment.
> NEWS LOUNGE ROOM — an informal area where reporters and news staff can relax with on-duty Media Committee members. Delegates are excluded unless invited by media representatives.
> NEWS ROOM — tables, chairs, manual and electric typewriters, speeches, biographies, photos, outside-line telephones, teletype, TV monitors, message board and a clock. Include ashtrays, water,

glasses, paper, wastepaper baskets, spare typewriter ribbons, pens and pencils. Long distance telephone calls must be settled on the spot.

DUPLICATING ROOM — pair this up with the Conference Information Center. Duplicating is important for last-minute speeches and releases. To avoid distraction, keep the duplication equipment away from the news facility.

Space for these five areas is vital. Recently reporters left a well-promoted major conference to cover a smaller convention in the same hotel, simply because the latter had better media facilities. If having five separate, but connecting, rooms is beyond the conference budget, one large room divided into the same five work areas is equally effective. The secret is to identify noisy and quiet areas so the media can work undisturbed.

Today effective pre-conference media relations should be almost an automatic process. When all media outlets have been surveyed, a letter or media kit should be prepared for distribution at least two weeks before the conference begins. Media kits should only be prepared to promote major conferences in large cities where other news events within the community make the competition for news coverage tough. Smaller conferences in less populated communities can often achieve full media impact by mailing out a letter giving the details.

Media kits should bear the conference logo, name, location and dates. Contents must be straightforward and crisp. Consider the following information material:

> Organization's nature and purpose
> Conference objectives and themes
> Conference program — in detail
> Speakers' biographies and photos
> Executives' biographies and photos
> VIP's biographies and photos
> Position papers, technical papers
> Detailed description of Media Committee room
> News conference schedule
> Media Committee names, addresses and telephone numbers.

Schedule news conferences once or twice a day: the first right after breakfast, the second immediately following lunch. The association executive usually wants delegates to get all the news first on the convention floor. The media doesn't work that way today. It cannot afford to cover your conference for four days in the hope that something interesting will happen. Reporters are busy people. Some radio reporters have several stories to cover per day, some have been on the go since 6:00 A.M. By all means provide newsworthy material and personalities to maintain continued operation.

Good coverage is hard to achieve in cities where everyone is competing for news opportunities. Do something different. Advise the media that all important speakers will be available at scheduled news conferences before they address the convention.

Follow news conferences up with newspaper and television feature interviews, in addition to hot-line radio shows. Don't overlook cablevision. Some stations will want to broadcast your entire proceedings for their viewing audience.

Arrange luncheon and dinner dates for journalists with VIPs, senior executives and leading spokesmen. Situations like these generate broader insight of association or industry objectives and encourage color reporting or background articles, all of which bring wider conference coverage.

Face reality — there is no definitive answer to the number of media representatives who should attend conference receptions. Some journalists obtain their best leads at these gatherings. In any case, all media should be invited to the opening, get-acquainted, and farewell gatherings.

Keep the media continuously informed before, during and after the conference. Your media action plan should be along the following lines:

FOLLOW-UP BEFORE: Phone enquiries for the following purposes: Did media kits get to right persons? Any more required? How many meal and reception tickets required? Any additional information necessary? Any interviews required? Are conference releases and photos required? Advise of last-minute changes and additions such as speakers or program.

FOLLOW-UP DURING: Media kits for late arrivals, conference badges and programs for all media representatives. Delegate listings and rosters. Coffee and sandwiches on hand during news-room hours. Speeches, photos and releases on hand at start of each news conference. VIP, speaker and executive contact service. Transportation for delivery of speeches, photos and releases.

FOLLOW-UP AFTER: Election of officers — releases, biographies and photos. Outgoing conference chairman's statement. Speeches, photos, releases to trade and business journals. News clipping service. Thank you letters to all media.

Consider an opening news conference at the local airport on the arrival of the national chairman or president. This symbolizes where first concerns really lie and generates good coverage. It is also the time to set up private interviews and ensure that the media feels welcome at all proceedings.

These opening news conferences provide the opportunity to review media facility hours and introduce the Media Committee staff. International congresses often plan to keep their facilities open day and night because news deadlines vary around the world. This means 24-hour staffing. Shifts should be held to six hour stints.

If your conference is national or local in nature, the media facility should open at 7:00 A.M. and close around 10:00 P.M. The closing can be earlier but always allow at least one hour after the last meeting of the day. Again, six-hour shifts should be enforced. Staff the media rooms with public relations-minded personnel at all times. They require in-depth background information on the organization and on the conference purposes.

It goes without saying that news conferences must start and stop on time. If speech material can be made available 24 hours before each news conference, so much the better. This gives feature and public affairs journalists an opportunity to get into the act. All news conferences should be moderated by an expert in the association, preferably a public relations official who knows what it is all about. Ensure that moderators are fluent in the official conference languages.

In dealing with the media, keep it short and simple, be factual and objective. Forget gifts for the media. Openness and cooperation count.

## MEDIA COMMITTEE CHECKLIST

Identify and catalogue all media outlets ☐
Develop media policies ☐
Prepare media relations program ☐
Prepare media kits and material ☐
Staff media facility with professional, informed people ☐
Order materials and equipment from Service Committee ☐
Arrange for coffee on continuous basis ☐
Determine staffing schedule ☐
Develop conference backgrounders ☐
Organize news conference schedule ☐
Distribute speech texts ☐
Attach biographies to every speech ☐
Set up photo services ☐
Hold advance news conferences ☐
Insure every news conference is newsworthy ☐
Run news conferences on time ☐
Determine media attendance policy for all events ☐

# 26

Total Planning –
# GLUING THE
# PIECES TOGETHER

**P**revious chapters have described the work of convention planning committees, their objectives and research tasks, their preliminary planning techniques and how they must coordinate with each other to eliminate overlaps. These chapters have detailed a conference planning structure where there is equal authority and where committee heads are expected to resolve as much as possible, without referral to the conference echelon.

Reviewing and resolving problems as a team provides excellent experience for operations on the convention floor. Several committees working together usually means clearer identification of responsibilities and encourages work trade offs to committees already undertaking similar tasks.

Up to this point, the function of the chairman, co-chairman, and the Executive Committee has been to ensure that committees are organized and operating according to plan. By now committees have developed full work schedules or checklists and should have resolved their common problems.

From this point on, data gathering and analysis must take a diminishing amount of committee effort. The time has come for the chairman and the Executive Committee to adopt a detailed plan for the management and operation of the convention itself. The object is not to print reams of instructions but to organize and manage a conference with a minimum of confusion and work.

The solution the authors have found most effective is to develop consolidated charts — one for each and every conference event. This will enable every conference worker to perform his or her specific function with a full knowledge of everyone's responsibility. Fortunately, these charts are easy to develop. Acquire copies of every working paper developed by each committee and rewrite them. Assign each event a number, in sequence. These numbers also provide account numbers for the Finance Committee.

Each consolidated chart precisely explains the requirements, mood and setting for every item on the conference program. It means detailed write-ups of the following material, along with deadline dates:

> Event number and name
> Date, time and location
> Sponsor
> Purpose of the event
> Description of room layout
> Budget — expenditure breakdown
> Head table guests — if necessary
> Menu
> Program timing
> Program script
> Events Committee responsibilities
> Program Committee responsibilities
> Speakers Committee responsibilities
> Service Committee responsibilities
> Registration Committee responsibilities
> Media Committee responsibilities
> Printing Committee responsibilities
> Youth Committee responsibilities
> Family Group Committee responsibilities
> Sponsor Committee responsibilities
> Accommodation Committee responsibilities
> Awards Committee responsibilities
> Display Committee responsibilities
> Transportation Committee responsibilities
> Finance Committee responsibilities.

Delete committees from each chart wherever these groups have no duties or responsibilities. If the charts are properly completed, a host of preliminary planning and organization material can now be filed. Remember, it is too expensive to provide everyone with full sets of operating papers for each conference item. So, make sure committee chairmen have as few staff on the convention floor as possible.

Further simplification is accomplished with the appointment of one person to a special conference role — the Event Leader. The Event Leader is the individual who checks each and every event 10, 15, or 20 minutes before it begins.

The Event Leader needs several qualifications to perform many complex tasks. Good leaders are busy people. They must resolve any committee conflicts which may arise on the conference floor. General problem solving by Event Leaders leaves major problems to the Conference Chairman and Co-chairman. The main responsibility of the Event Leader is to start and stop everything on time.

The path to conference success is paved with good intentions. It takes an Event Leader with power over every Committee Chairman to translate these intentions into deeds. If you can arrange and manage a tight conference schedule, delegates will be pleased and pleasantly surprised!

Appoint one Head-Table Coordinator for the entire conference to further reinforce your decision to manage with confidence. Too much is left to chance if place-card settings are the responsibility of one person, head table lineups a second person's task and so on.

Head-Table Coordinators must be calm individuals and so efficient they are admired by everyone. Your Coordinator should be responsible for all head-table arrangements, such as head-table settings, gatherings, place cards, lineups, entries and final seating. He or she checks that all head-table mikes are operating a few moments before each event begins. And the Coordinator has spare copies of speeches, scripts and event charts in reserve.

These consolidated event charts should be prepared by the Co-Chairman. Give one copy of each chart to the hotel manager, with his or her responsibilities underlined in red. It's the secret to top-notch liaison throughout the convention. A completed chart for the twelfth event on Thursday, July 10 and the seventeenth event on the same day shown in this example gives an idea of the format.

**EVENT 10 - 12**
**CONFERENCE ARRANGEMENTS AND RESPONSIBILITIES**

THURSDAY, JULY 10, 19
2:00 PM - 5:00 PM: PROMOTION SESSIONS
SPONSORS: GENERAL CONFERENCE FUNDS
LOCATIONS: MANAGEMENT IN THE '80s, CRYSTAL BALLROOM
   2nd FLOOR, BENSON BAY HOTEL
PROMOTIONS ASSOCIATION AND YOU, EXHIBIT
   LOUNGE, 2nd FLOOR, BENSON BAY HOTEL

ENVIRONMENT AND PEOPLE, HUNT ROOM,
2nd FLOOR, BENSON BAY HOTEL
EDUCATION FOR TOMORROW, HOUND ROOM
2nd FLOOR, BENSON BAY HOTEL

PURPOSE:

Four concurrent sessions — delegates can attend as many as three meetings on an individual basis.

BUDGET:

$400. MAXIMUM — sound systems and room signs, coffee break.

ROOMS:

CRYSTAL BALLROOM AND ALSO EXHIBIT LOUNGE

Area set up in Crystal Ballroom — one head table, white cloth, paper, ashtrays, water glasses, pencils, three chairs. Theatre-style audience, 100 chairs, facing head table, scattered ashtrays. Small table at door for event ticket deposit. One lectern for head table. Five table mikes, four floor mikes, and sound system with operator. Similar area set up in Exhibit Lounge.

HUNT ROOM AND ALSO HOUND ROOM

Area set up in Hunt Room — one head table, white cloth, paper, ashtrays, water, glasses, pencils, three chairs, Theatre-style audience, 75 chairs facing head table, adequate ash trays. Small table at door for event ticket deposit. One lectern (without sound) for head table. Three table mikes and sound system. Similar area set up in Hound Room. Coffee breaks in all four areas.

PROGRAM:

2:00 PM Each session commences
2:30 PM Each session concludes
2:30 PM Each session commences
3:00 PM Each session concludes
3:00 PM Coffee break in each session room
3:30 PM Each coffee break concludes
3:30 PM Each session commences
4:00 PM Each session concludes

SPEAKERS:

MANAGEMENT IN THE '80s: Ronald Grant and Eric Stephens.
Martha Franks, Moderator.

SPEAKERS:

THE ASSOCIATION AND YOU: Don Hamilton and Monty Berrigan
Moderator.

SPEAKERS:

ENVIRONMENT AND PEOPLE: Tom Sherman and Lynn Dogood.
Andrea Arnett, Moderator.

SPEAKERS:

EDUCATION FOR TOMORROW: Prof. Bill Scott.
Ruth Johnson, Moderator.

COMMITTEES:

SPEAKERS (Pre-Conference)

—Complete names all session speakers, six months prior to event.
—Complete names all panelists, six months prior to event.
—Complete names all session moderators, six months prior to event.
—Advise SERVICES Committee of all requirements, six months prior
 to event.
—Advise PRINTING Committee of all requirements, six months
 prior to event.
—Complete all session topics and arrangements, five months prior
 to event.
—Advise PROMOTION Committee all details, five months prior
 to event.
—Copies of confirmation letters to session speakers, panelists,
 moderators, four months prior to event.
—Advise EXHIBIT Committee of all requirements, one month prior
 to event.
—Confirm room set-ups to SERVICES Committee.
—Confirm room locations to EVENTS Committee.
—Conduct rehearsal sessions day prior to event.
—Ensure moderators and panelists on hand day prior to event.
—Monitor each session, ensure each concludes at proper times.
—Obtain attendance count for coffee to BUDGET and to Hotel.
—Obtain all event tickets at doors, turn in to EVENTS Committee.
SERVICES
—Provide furniture set-ups to Hotel, one month prior to event.
—Supply sound systems if required, with a minimum of one mike
 for every speaker, panelist, moderator.
—Supply one operator to monitor every individual system.
—Supply head table place cards as required.
—Supply film and slide projectors with screens as required.
—Obtain signs from EXHIBIT and PRINTING Committees.
—Erect signs 1:45 PM, day of event.
—Supply paper, pencils, etc., for each head table.
—Remove and store or return all equipment at end of event.
EXHIBITS
—Provide room signs as required to SERVICES Committee, day
 prior to event.
PRINTING
—Provide speakers', panelists' and moderators' table identification
 cards as required, day prior to event.
MEDIA
—Supply photographer to shoot Promotion Session in Crystal
 Ballroom.
—Prepare cutlines and item for Promotions Association International
 Magazine.
—Confirm SPEAKERS Committee arrangements twice, one month
 and again one day prior to event.
—Confirm SERVICE Committee arrangements twice, as above.
—Confirm EXHIBITS Committee arrangements twice.

—Confirm PRINTING Committee arrangements twice.
—Confirm MEDIA Committee arrangements twice.
—Confirm EVENTS Committee arrangements twice.
—Confirm all room set-ups in place 1:45 PM, July 10.
—Ensure coffee breaks exactly on time.
—Ensure programs run as scheduled.
EVENTS
—Reconfirm room location with Hotel four months prior to event.
—Ensure room set-up in place by 1:45 PM, July 10.
—Confirm coffee break and coffee count to Hotel.
FINANCE
BUDGET ACCOUNT 10 - 12
—Confirm SPEAKERS Committee budget expense twice, six months
    and again one month prior to event.
—Confirm SERVICES Committee budget expense twice, as above.
—Confirm EXHIBITS Committee budget expense twice.
—Confirm PRINTING Committee budget expense twice.
—Confirm MEDIA Committee budget expense twice.
—Confirm EVENTS Committee budget expense twice.
—Obtain coffee counts from EVENTS Committee, July 10.
—Accept and pay necessary invoices within budget after event.

## EVENT 10 - 17
## CONFERENCE ARRANGEMENTS AND RESPONSIBILITIES
THURSDAY, JULY 10, 19—
7:00 PM - 9:00 PM: NATIONAL AWARDS DINNER
SPONSORS: FEDERAL STATE INSURANCE and THE AUSTRIAN
    WINE CONGRESS
LOCATION: LOGAN ROOM, MAIN FLOOR, BENSON BAY HOTEL

PURPOSE:

Presentation of SERVICE AWARD, ATTAINMENT AWARD, THE
PUBLIC SERVICE SHIELD and speech by DAWN RICE, DIRECTOR,
PUBLIC RELATIONS, WARNER CORPORATION, CHICAGO, for all
delegates, spouses and children. Entertainment by David King and
The Public Opinion. PROMOTION IN THE 80s wine glasses to
be placed at every table setting.

BUDGET:

$3,000. MAXIMUM, including meal, head table place cards, head
table and audience table flowers, sound rental, wine glasses,
entertainment, tax and tip. Wines supplied by AUSTRIAN WINE
CONGRESS.

ROOM:

Logan Room arranged banquet-style. Head table 9 places on
platform (raised one foot along west wall of room). Audience to
be seated at eight-place round tables, white cloths. Small registration
desk and chair outside entrance door. Three head table mikes.
Lectern, if required by speaker. Flowers on head table and
audience tables. Platform at north west end of room for orchestra.

MENU:

    NOTE: HAM MUST BE OLD FASHIONED, SUGAR CURED, NOT PRE-COOKED OR ROLLED.

    Celery and Olives
    Yellow Pea Soup, Quebecoise
    Baked Ham, Orange Sauce, Glazed Pineapple, Crabapple slice
    Au Gratin Potatoes
    Broccoli Au Beurre
    Tossed Green Salad             400 Plates @ $5.50
    Rolls and Butter               20 Plates @ $4.00
    Cheese-Board Selection
    Cracker Selection
    Coffee - Tea - Milk
    SPECIAL NOTE: - *Special Childrens' Dessert to be served in Hunt Room, Benson Bay Hotel. Cost included in menu. See event 10-18: Austrian Film Fun.*

WINES:

    DINNER
    Trocken Moselle
    Lenz Eden Valley
    Edelweiss Sauternes
    Eschenauer Burgundy
    Blue Nun Pearl

WINES:

    DESSERT
    Trocken Golden Cream
    Eschenauer Reserve
    Austria Blonde
    Hapsburg Fine Old Sherry

HEAD TABLE:

    CHAIRMAN'S LEFT TO RIGHT
    Mrs. Paul Monson
    Mr. Kent Montcreif, Austrian Wine Congress Host
    Mrs. Greg Burton
    Ms. Dawn Rice, Dinner Speaker
    Mr. Lee MacNeil, Dinner Chairman
    Mrs. Lee MacNeil
    Mr. Greg Burton, Awards Chairman
    Mrs. Kent Montcreif
    Mr. Paul Monson, Federal State Insurance Host

PROGRAM:

    6:30 PM Ensure wine glasses are clean and in place.
    6:50 PM Staff registration desk at door.
    6:50 PM Accept event tickets at door, obtain attendance count.
    6:50 PM Head Table assembles in Media Lounge, Second Floor, Benson Bay Hotel
    6:55 PM Entertainment begins.
    7:00 PM Event begins, random seating.

7:00 PM Side dishes pre-set at tables.
7:05 PM Parade to "SPEAKER'S RIGHT SIDE OF TABLE".
7:05 PM Entertainment Pause.
7:05 PM Chairman's Opening Remarks, Presentation of Wine
     Glasses, Grace, Toasts.
7:08 PM Chairman concludes.
7:08 PM Entertainment Commences.
7:10 PM Soup course served.
7:20 PM Main course served.
7:50 PM Entertainment pauses.
7:50 PM Chairman introduces Head Table.
7:55 PM Chairman concludes.
7:58 PM Chairman introduces Awards Chairman.
8:00 PM Awards Presentation — AWARDS CHAIRMAN.
8:00 PM Photographs each award.
8:15 PM Awards Presentation concludes.
8:15 PM Children depart to Hunt Room.
8:15 PM Entertainment March for children.
8:18 PM Chairman introduces Dinner Speaker.
8:20 PM Speech — Dawn Rice
9:00 PM Speech concludes.
9:00 PM Chairman thanks Rice, makes presentation.
9:00 PM Cheese and wine served all tables.
9:00 PM Entertainment recommences.
9:15 PM Coffee served all tables.
9:25 PM Chairman thanks audience and co-sponsors.
9:30 PM Event concludes.

COMMITTEES:

EVENTS

—Confirm head table guests available, two months prior to event.
—Confirm Dinner Chairman, two months prior to event.
—Confirm room location with Hotel.
—Confirm menu and costs arrangements with Hotel.
—Confirm room set-up with Hotel.
—Prepare head table guest list according to seating.
—Accept event tickets from Speakers Commitee.
—Remind all Head Table of attendance, by letter, advise to
 assemble in Media Lounge.
—Obtain two ushers — in period costume.
—Ensure entertainment on hand, July 9.
—Confirm wine arrangements with Austrian Wine Congress.
—Confirm attendance count to BUDGET Committee and Hotel.

SPEAKERS

—Purchase mementos for Speaker and Wife.
—Obtain Speaker's biographic material and photos, two months
 prior to event.
—Prepare script for dinner chairman, one month prior to event.
—Deliver biography material and speech to MEDIA Committee,

one month prior to event.

—Deliver mementos and script to Dinner Chairman, two weeks prior to event.

—Ensure Speaker in Media Lounge, 6:50 PM, July 10.

—Deliver AWARDS Committee script to Dinner Chairman, two weeks prior to event.

## HEAD TABLE COORDINATOR

—Confirm Head Table guests, obtain final seating list, June 10.

—Inform all Head Table guests to meet in Media Lounge, July 10.

—Obtain final check on Head Table seating list and place cards from EVENTS Committee, 6:00 PM, July 10.

—Final check Head Table mikes, set place cards, 6:45 PM, July 10.

—Assemble Head Table guests in Media Lounge, 6:50 PM, July 10.

—Obtain event tickets from Head Table guests, have spares on hand

—Line up Head Table guests in Media Lounge according to place cards and seating list.

—Turn in Head Table guest tickets at door.

—Announce Head Table at door.

—Lead Head Table parade to assigned seats at 7:05 PM, July 10.

—Lead parade to SPEAKER'S RIGHT end of table.

—Have spare Chairman's script and dinner speech available.

## SERVICES

—Confirm furniture set-up with Hotel.

—Supply banners behind Head Table.

—Platform and chairs at northwest end of room as required by band.

—Head Table platform on west wall of room — 10 place settings.

—Supply flowers to Head Table every four feet.

—Supply flowers to all audience tables.

—Supply three Head Table mikes and operator.

—Supply lectern if required by speaker.

—Remove Head Table mikes at end of event.

## PRINTING

—Prepare hand-lettered place cards for Head Table.

—Deliver to Head Table Coordinator.

## ENTERTAINMENT

—Provide entertainment by six-piece orchestra, obtain costs.

—Provide all equipment necessary for orchestra.

—Orchestra advised of final program by EVENTS Committee.

## MEDIA

—Supply photographer for Awards Presentations.

—Prepare photos and item for media.

## AWARDS

—Obtain necessary awards, two months prior to event.

—Select awards candidates as required, one month prior to event.

—Advise awards winners time and place of presentation.

—Obtain biographies, media material, two weeks prior to event.

—Advise MEDIA Committee of awards selection, two weeks prior to event.

—Deliver biographies, media material to MEDIA Committee, two weeks prior to event.

—Prepare AWARDS Script, deliver to SPEAKERS Committee, two weeks prior to event.

PROGRAM

—Confirm EVENTS Committee arrangements twice, one month and again one day prior to event.

—Confirm SPEAKERS Committee arrangements twice, as above.

—Confirm ENTERTAINMENT Committee arrangements twice.

—Confirm SERVICES Committee arrangements twice.

—Confirm PRINTING Committee arrangements twice.

—Confirm ENTERTAINMENT Committee arrangements twice.

—Confirm MEDIA Committee arrangements twice.

—Confirm AWARDS Committee arrangements twice.

—Ensure room set-up in place by 6:30 PM, July 10.

—Ensure Head Table on hand 6:50 PM, July 10.

—Ensure Head Table Coordinator has all material on hand.

—Ensure program runs as scheduled.

FINANCE

BUDGET ACCOUNT 10-17

—Confirm EVENTS Committee budget expense twice, six months and again one month prior to event.

—Confirm SPEAKERS Committee budget expense twice.

—Confirm SERVICES Committee budget expense twice.

—Confirm PRINTING Committee budget expense twice.

—Confirm ENTERTAINMENT Committee budget expense twice.

—Confirm MEDIA Committee budget expense twice.

—Confirm AWARDS Committee budget expense twice.

—Confirm attendance count with EVENTS Committee, July 10.

—Accept and pay necessary invoices within budget after event.

# 27

What To Do –
## BEFORE IT'S TOO LATE

**T**he week before the conference is absolutely vital to ensuring success. The Finance Committee must do a final expense and revenue review and advise the Executive Committee of the sponsor situation. There is still time to cut back on certain events to stay within the overall convention budget. The Exhibits Committee will still be completing Exhibit Lounge space allocations, making certain the majority of exhibits have been received and that the display company is ready to go. Most of the staff from the Publicity and Printing Committees are now working on the Media Committee, providing assistance where it counts. Services and Equipment, as well as the Transportation group are swinging into action. Every item of equipment and transportation is being double checked for availability and reliability.

Meanwhile Accommodation, Registration, Information and Hosting groups are holding dry runs so everything will be second nature in the hectic days ahead. Hotel rooms are at a premium yet last-minute registrations still trickle in, causing extra work for staff who are nevertheless determined to get good accommodation for every registrant.

SUCCESSFUL CONFERENCE & CONVENTION PLANNING

Schedule a dry run of the registration operation during a quiet period only in the pre-conference week. You will soon learn what things aren't working as originally planned. These buffer days mean time to perfect new systems if that's what is needed.

All committees in the Program Group—Events, Entertainment, Program, Speakers, Youth, Family—should now be operating as a Committee-of-the-Whole. Coordinated checking at this stage should resolve speaker no shows and tighten up sessions. It means solving minor problems before they get out of hand. For instance, a major entertainer cancels out and is replaced by a new overnight sensation, whose price is still realistic. A small ballroom for the teen lounge has been double-booked, the hotel offers a vacant VIP suite in exchange.

The Exhibit Committee has the convention Display Board altered to show the new teen lounge location. It prepares new place cards for the Head Table Coordinator. The Speakers Committee meanwhile makes any necessary changes in the chairman's and moderator's scripts.

Two days before the conference begins, open the hospitality center, receiving room and information office. Although nothing is happening on the surface, exhibits and displays are beginning to arrive. Equipment and office supplies may be piling up in several hotel nooks and crannies. Convention kits and delegate materials must be stored in a safe location. Several committees are already in action at the hotel and would appreciate a temporary base of operations.

On the last regular work day before the convention, the conference chairman calls a meeting of the entire committee staff. Out-of-town committee members are urged to attend. All events are reviewed. People have been assigned to perform each function on the consolidated event charts. The potential danger of communication blocks is explored. Staff is praised for acting on individual initiative and encouraged to do more of the same. Essentially, this meeting is best thought of as an "Any Problems?" session, to bring out possible weaknesses or defects and resolve them then and there.

Once "problems" have been cleared at the meeting the Executive Committee and committee chairman must meet with the hotel executive —the manager and all his department heads—to complete the convention dry run. By now, the hotel staff will be fully in the picture—the hotel copies of the consolidated event charts will see to that. If homework has been well done, this meeting should take less than 90 minutes.

It is also a good time for the chairman and co-chairman to move into the hotel. Most of the remaining conference decisions are focused in the hotel itself. Establish yourself there and deal with these items on a personal basis.

Open the formal Registration Center the day before the conference begins, to satisfy everyone it works without snags. A noon-hour opening is best. Keep it staffed until 9:00 P.M. or one hour after the early arrival reception.

These receptions, held in the evening before the conference gets under way, are more than just ice breakers for delegates, speakers, sponsors and committee workers. Advance get-acquainted sessions are usually small gatherings. It means the conference committee can evaluate the hotel operation and itself.

If comittee planning or hotel services fall somewhat short of expectations, the committee chairmen and the Executive Committee still have 12 hours to ensure smooth-running functions. After the reception is over, hold a 20-minute review with the committee chairmen—but only if there are problems. Otherwise, stay calm and relaxed.

The fewer committee meetings during the conference the better. That is why you appointed an Event Leader and a Head Table Coordinator. You and your co-chairman have long since made all your plans. Now you are free to roam the conference floor, checking, checking, checking behind the scenes. Each morning, 10 or 20 minutes before breakfast, discuss with each committee chairman any questionable situations. Apart from that, stay out of the way and let the workers get on with their jobs. Don't overlook checking the hotel notice board. If you are the North American Promotion Association and you have been abbreviated as North American Promo Ass—it could be embarrassing.

Your duties should change very little during each conference day. Early rising, a quick walk through the entire convention hotel, early committee chairmen discussions to iron out yesterday's wrinkles and a continued policy of the Event Leader ruling the roost. Keep tabs on event head counts as well. A wrong count during an early event is a good omen. It demonstrates few items can be left to chance.

Many other incidents, too numerous to catalogue, can be expected during the actual conference. Even if they could be elaborated in full detail for the exacting conference planner, they would not be complete, because new difficulties crop up every day as more hotels open and more conferences and conventions take place.

But that's the reason for all the detailed conference planning—to minimize chaos, to get known difficulties out of the way and to organize people so that the conference chairman and co-chairman can worry out the new unknowns.

Not to be forgotten are the other more important reasons for conference planning—to guarantee events start and stop on time and to conclude the convention with at least $1.00 surplus. More, if that is the goal. And, if you have followed suggestions up to this point and have event sponsors, you should be able to realize a profit of up to $10.00 per delegate, based on a $150.00 full-board registration fee—together with one or two free receptions!

# 28

It's All Over But –
# AUDITING AND EVALUATING

**R**eserve the last day for conference farewells. It is important that every conference committee member is personally thanked by his or her chairman, the conference chairman and the co-chairman. Thank you letters are also required, but a thank you in person means much more, particularly if everyone is basking in success.

Often overlooked, but very necessary, is the business of getting delegates out of the conference hotel. When everyone is gone, when all the conference paraphernalia is out of the hotel, invite the manager to the conference suite and thank him or her sincerely. Make special mention of excellent service and any particular courtesies. Turn in your keys, head home and relax for 24 hours. You deserve it—moreover the rest is necessary as the job is still not finished.

It is a pity people who have worked so hard and so long can't forget the whole affair for at least a month. But life—and conferences—seldom work out that way. Two committees must swing into action immediately before the job can be considered complete. The Post-Conference Committee backed up by Publicity and Media staff, must begin to publish and distribute the complete record to all organization members as well as to the delegates. The convention documents must provide a description of the proceedings, cover the content and structure of each session, contain basic conference papers and furnish an interesting digest of conference results. Constitutional amendments and by-law revisions are included, if relevant to the convention.

Finance is now operating at highest gear, settling bills and invoices, as well as getting firm about any outstanding donations or revenue. There are also delegate refunds to settle—reimbursements to those who couldn't attend at the last moment for valid reasons. If the conference is operating well in the black make refunds without hesitation as it is good public relations.

Finance is also in a huddle with the auditor. Hopefully, his or her instructions have been followed to the letter during the last few months. Even if auditor services were not required in the past, insist on a professional audit for your convention. The expense will be minimal and there should be no complaints with a formal audited statement. The point is that the conference is *only* officially complete when the auditor's seal is on the financial statement.

Keep accounting simple. The forms suggested here demonstrate the less complicated the system, the easier it is to manage and understand.

Landmark

To The National Executive,
North American Promotions Association
AUDIT REPORT

I have examined the transactions of the North American Promotions Association, Promotion in the 80s Convention.

The detailed records of revenue for sponsors' cash contributions, registration fees and miscellaneous credits are accurate and the statement of receipts and disbursements presents fairly the financial position of the convention.

I also confirm that bank deposits totalled $............. and that in my opinion, the disbursements present fairly the expenses paid on behalf of the convention. The formal audit confirms that a surplus of $................ is on hand at the conclusion of the auditing of the conference accounts.

L. J. Simpson, C.A.
October 21, 19—.

RECEIPTS & DISBURSEMENTS FOR PROMOTIONS IN THE 80s CONFERENCE

*Receipts:*

| | | |
|---|---:|---:|
| Sponsors' Cash Contributions | $ 21,207.38 | |
| Registration Fees | 32,306.50 | |
| Booth Sponsorships (Space Rental) | 5,700.00 | |
| Miscellaneous Credits (sale of boat tickets, draws, individual dinner tickets, etc. | 2,900.77 | |
| Interest on Term Deposit | 308.74 | |
| National Association Advance | 3,000.00 | |
| Local Association Advance | 1,500.00 | $ 66,923.39 |

*Disbursements:*

| | | |
|---|---:|---:|
| Printing and Stationery | $ 4,921.92 | |
| Registration Refunds | 2,585.00 | |
| Photography | 487.50 | |
| Landmark Star Cruise | 2,100.00 | |
| Lemoine Park 'Zoo Doo' | 1,318.58 | |
| Miscellaneous Transportation | 2,827.50 | |
| Musical Entertainment, P.A. System, Background Music | 991.45 | |
| Benson Bay Hotel: (meals, rooms, gratuity, tax, etc.) | 27,144.08 | |
| Gifts for Speakers | 514.20 | |
| Speaker Fees and Expenses | 6,194.58 | |
| Convention Staff | 1,236.05 | |
| Insurance Costs | 130.00 | |
| Flowers (corsages, arrangements) | 1,135.45 | |
| Other Conference Expenses (wine glasses, telephone, extra staff, committee meeting expenses, advertising and exhibits) | 3,963.20 | |
| Auditor and Consultant Fees | 2,170.00 | |
| National Association Advance | 3,000.00 | |
| Local Association Advance | 1,500.00 | $ 62,219.51 |
| BALANCE ON HAND | | $ 4,703.88 |

Now that the conference is over, turn to the evaluation. There are more ways to evaluate conferences and conventions than most people imagine. Generally, evaluators should limit research to the following basics:

Were conference objectives and goals achieved?

> Delegate goals and objectives
> Association goals and objectives
> General public goals and objectives
> Committee goals and objectives

What are the actual effects?

> Immediate
> Short-term
> Long-term

What was the actual value of the conference?

> Was it worth the time, energy and expense?
> Has there been a beneficial effect?

What was the delegate satisfaction quotient?

> Were delegates pleased with conference arrangements?
> Were delegates satisfied with conference accommodations?
> Were delegates hosted properly by conference committees?

What was the work session impact?

> Evaluation of group and plenary sessions.
> Evaluation of speakers and panelists.
> Evaluation of relevance factors.

Evaluation is valuable when delegates voice opinions in an organized manner. Responsible assessments become guidelines for change and improvement at future conventions. The type of delegate feedback you should be soliciting is detailed in Chapter 3.

Who should evaluate the convention? This depends on the complexity of the conference objectives and goals. If the organization is in the midst of major technological change, for example, research experts are required. Contact them before the conference begins and let them recommend a program which is financially acceptable to the association and the conference budget.

Most convention planners rely on their own Post-Conference Committee to devise session and program evaluation techniques. Whether professional experts or committee members are involved, eliminate bias factors in the survey material. Questions have to be so phrased that they do not seem to invite a particular answer. Committee members, in analyzing the response data, have to write objective reports. If that cannot be managed, then evaluation becomes a waste of time and money.

Confine your evaluations to Attendance Audits, Audience Interest Questionnaires and Reaction Forms.

> ATTENDANCE AUDITS: Measure who attended and why, what management level was represented, number of repeaters, value of technical sessions and number of attendees per session.

> AUDIENCE INTEREST QUESTIONNAIRES: Like Attendance, Audit Forms are circulated during the conference proceedings. Information sought includes age group, business classification, management level

and general opinions on the total program rather than individual sessions.

REACTION FORMS: Distributed by mail one day to one month after the conference concludes. Skilled researchers can interpret random samples quite effectively and provide valid survey information. Most Post-Conference Committees will probably not have the necessary expertise to accurately assess random survey results and so total universe surveys would be more suitable.

A two-page survey limited to 15 questions is more than sufficient. Beyond that, respondent attention diminishes appreciably and in all probability the extra questions are not eliciting useful information. A survey could be developed along the following lines with a five-point evaluation scale to cut down open-end response. The examples given here offer a typical format:

- The program as a whole was Stimulating————— Unusual————— Ordinary————— Boring————— Dull—————

- The program content as a whole was Informative————— Worthwhile————— Ordinary————— Too General————— Waste of my time—————

- Evaluation of major speaker Dawn Rice: "Promotions and the body of knowledge" was Stimulating—————· Informative————— Ordinary————— Uninformative————— Waste of my time—————

Other types of audience surveys are often useful, particularly if there is a cause to evaluate the conference environment and delegate reaction to food, refreshment and accommodation. But audience profile techniques can be quite complicated and it is advisable to seek expert help to ensure the answers are worth getting in the first place. Herein lies the real reason for demanding professional evaluation techniques as an essential element of the convention. How did the conference come about in the first place? It had to be for one of the reasons outlined in the opening chapters—to pool information, to achieve group decisions, to educate, to clarify issues, to develop policy, to negotiate, to offer rewards or to seek support.

If the evaluation process statistically demonstrates beyond doubt that these goals have been realized you have run a successful convention. It was worth it after all.

## POST CONVENTION CHECKLIST

Establish evaluation policy and staff ☐
Receive Finance Comittee audited statements ☐
Distribute statements to delegates and membership ☐
Receive taped proceedings from Services Committee ☐

Transcribe and edit proceedings ☐
Distribute proceedings to delegates, membership and press ☐
Develop thank you letter list ☐
Distribute thank you letters ☐
Complete evaluation policy ☐
Prepare and collect post-conference survey forms ☐
Evaluate post-conference surveys ☐
Prepare brief report for delegates and membership ☐
Distribute to delegates and membership ☐
Prepare and distribute detailed report for Association
   Executive and next year's convention hosts ☐

# Bibliography

Bieber, Marion, *How To Run A Conference*, Fernhill, 1968.

Canadian Government Travel Bureau, *Proceedings, First Canadian Convention Seminar*, Canadian Government Travel Bureau, Ottawa, 1968.

Canadian Government Travel Bureau, *Proceedings, Second Canadian Convention Seminar*, Canadian Government Travel Bureau, Ottawa, 1969.

Canadian Government Travel Bureau, *Proceedings, Third Canadian Convention Seminar*, Canadian Government Travel Bureau, Ottawa, 1970.

Dun & Bradstreet Business Library, *How To Conduct A Meeting* (paperback), Thomas Y. Crowell, New York, 1970. Apollo Editions, Inc., New York, 1970.

Financial Post, *Report On Conventions* (tabloid), Maclean-Hunter Ltd., Toronto, December 1970 and August 1971.

Gray, Walter Jr., *Manual For Discussion Moderators* (paperback), American Institute of Discussions, 1964.

Hegarty, Edward J., *How To Run Better Meetings*, McGraw-Hill Inc., New York, 1957.

International Association of Convention Bureaus, *Convention Delegate Expenditures*, (paperback), International Association of Convention Bureaus, Cincinatti, Ohio, 1967.

International Association of Convention Bureaus, *Convention Liaison Manual*, International Association of Convention Bureaus, Cincinatti, Ohio, 1961.

International Association of Convention Bureaus, *Conventions, An American Institution* (paperback), International Association of Convention Bureaus, Cincinatti, Ohio, 1958.

International Union of Official Travel Organizations, *IUOTO Technical Bulletin*, International Union of Official Travel Organizations, Geneva, Switzerland, 1972.

Lobsenz, A. and Nicholas, G. P., "Symposiums, A Guide To Sponsorship", Public Relations Journal, 1968.

BIBLIOGRAPHY

Long, Fern, *All About Meetings,* Oceana Publications Inc., Dobbs Ferry, N.Y., 1967.

Marketing Magazine, *Conventions* (magazine), Maclean-Hunter Ltd., Toronto, Feb. 8, 1971 and Feb. 7, 1972.

Morgan, John S., *Political Guide To Conference Leadership,* McGraw-Hill Inc., New York, 1966.

National Education Association, Department of Classroom Teachers, *Handbook For Regional Conference Planner* (paperback), National Education Association Publishing, Washington, D.C., 1967.

Nilski, Therese, *Conference Interpretation In Canada* (paperback), Queen's Printer for Canada, Ottawa, 1969.

Parker, Jack T., *Running A Meeting,* Quick and Easy Series, Collier-MacMillan Canada Ltd., Toronto, 1963.

Sales Meeting Magazine, *Conferences* (magazine), Bill Publications, Philadelphia, Pa., 1969.

Sattler, William M. and W. Miller, *Discussion And Conference,* Second Edition 1968, Prentice-Hall Inc., Englewood Cliffs, N.J.

Shepherd, W. G., *How To Capitalize On Committees,* Textile World, 1967.

Snell, Frank, *How To Hold A Better Meeting,* Cornerstone Library Inc., New York, 1968.

Stanford, Geoffrey H., *Conduct Of Meetings,* Oxford University Press, Toronto, 1958.

Trans-World Airlines, *Conference Planners Handbook* (paperback), Trans-World Airlines, New York, 1971.

Utterback, William E., *Group Thinking and Conference Leadership,* Revised edition, 1964.

Whipps, R. C., *Commercial Conference Management,* Cahners Books International Inc., Boston, Mass., 1969.

# Index